CONNECTION LOST

AN ALTERNATIVE VIEW ON THE WORLD AS WE KNOW IT

M. REINBERG

the Peppertree Press
Sarasota, Florida

Copyright © M. Reinberg, 2014

All rights reserved. Published by the Peppertree Press, LLC. the Peppertree Press and associated logos are trademarks of the Peppertree Press, LLC.

No part of this publication may be reproduced, stored in a retrieval system, transmitted in any form or by any means, electronic, mechanical, photocopying, recording, or otherwise, without prior written permission of the publisher and author/illustrator. Graphic design by Rebecca Barbier.

For information regarding permission,
call 941-922-2662 or contact us at our website:
www.peppertreepublishing.com or write to:
the Peppertree Press, LLC.
Attention: Publisher
1269 First Street, Suite 7
Sarasota, Florida 34236

ISBN: 978-1-61493-299-4

Library of Congress Number: 2014918572

Printed in the U.S.A.

Printed October 2014

This book is dedicated to
Peter Joseph Hicks and Dusten Quillen.

The purpose of "Connection Lost" is to focus on things in society that attribute to, or lead to the destruction of our human connection to one another.

OVERVIEW	VII
RELIGION AND IDEOLOGY	1
WAR AND CONSEQUENCE	11
THE MISUSE OF POWER	22
POLITICS AND WEDGE ISSUES	32
A CULTURE OF SELF	43
INFECTION OF HATRED	53
THE ILLUSION OF SOCIAL CLASS AND STATUS	64
ENVIRONMENT AND RESOURCES	73
CONNECTION IGNORED	83
DIVIDED WE STAND	89
ENLIGHTENED	99
TECHNOLOGY AND SOCIAL MEDIA	107
OUR MONETARY SYSTEMS AND HUMAN ADVANCEMENT	110

OVERVIEW

Religion and Ideologies close our minds to alternative solutions, or viewpoints that cross cultural lines. The consequences of war regardless of "Why" last for generations and negatively impact everyone involved; there is no real winner in war. The misuse of power by people and leaders in high positions alienates society into distrust of government and leadership. Politics and Wedge issues are used against us to further divide us into conflicts of opinions and ideals. Corporations are valued and favored over people. Our culture pits us against each other in a false sense of competition that leads to selfish endeavors. All of this opens the flood gates to negativity and hatred. The illusion of social class and status lets money divide us. All of our tangible connections are ignored because they are clouded by all of these things. In the midst of this we stand divided, but if we open our minds we will be enlightened. Only then will we be truly united, and overcome these many segregations that have plagued mankind for thousands of years. Without all of these distractions we will realize that our true collective potential has absolutely no fathomable limits.

RELIGION AND IDEOLOGY

I USED TO GO TO CHURCH. I WAS AFRAID OF DYING and going to hell. I was afraid of being weak or being judged. This fear drove my motivation. So I read and studied the Bible until I knew every book in order. I memorized every verse that touched my heart. I had a righteousness that made me feel special. I felt like I had a purpose. It was simple. Pray and trust in god and I would go to heaven when I died. I segregated my mind from the facts of history and science. I looked down on people and attempted to convert them from other religions. I was segregated from the world in divine holiness. But what difference was I making? Unknowingly, I was doing my part in segregation that was no different than white or black segregation. I disregarded history, culture, and science in favor of fear.

My mission was to get to heaven. How many others have this mission? I realized at a young age that the type of mindset I possessed was exactly what was wrong with the world. We sever the ties with our fellow man before we even understand them. We put our psyches in a box that cannot be opened. With all of the different cultures and religions that are closed off to one another this is exactly why the world is as it seems today. A world cluttered with war and greed. Everyone thinks they have it all figured out. Religion became a weapon of mass destruction for me. It ensures that closed minds stay closed. It creates a false comfort or understanding.

I realized as long as I subscribed to my righteousness I would never be free to truly love the world. To love and understand everyone became my new mission. I began to question a lot choices I made based on my religion. As I learned about the beauty of other religions and cultures I realized how small my mind had been at one point in my life, but also how fragile all of our minds are. To read a book of any kind written by men and only believe what is written in that book is dangerous. I realized that a god would not confuse the world with a bunch of books or praise men for writing one or interpreting it to the masses. I realized that the only thing that mattered is that we love each other. Not only love each other, but understand each other. The Bible eventually became nothing but pollution to me.

There are so many different countries and regions all over the world that obviously lead to our cultural and religious diversity. Inherently having so much diversity and distance it should be expected that there will be a vast difference in beliefs, traditions, and ideologies. But our beliefs have lead to wars and social conflicts that still plague us today. There have been debates and arguments about what religion is the "right" religion, or who "god's" chosen people are that follow a specific religion. A separatist mindset has been a large cause of global acceptance to other cultures and religions. A primitive viewpoint of non-acceptance of other cultures is one of the main reasons conflict and cultural segregation are still a major problem around the world today.

One major example of pointless religious conflicts that lead to horrible segregation is the Christian and Muslim conflict in the African nation of Nigeria. Muslim extremists are bombing Christian churches and slaughtering women and children in their homes. These kinds of things are also going on in many other countries around the world involving other religions. Killing someone because of their culture or tradition is completely mindless, and barbaric. There has to be a mindset of reason and acceptance, or else no group or country can call themselves civilized.

The domestic and international segregation of religion and ideals has to end. Teaching or suggesting that people from other religions or belief systems stay away from each other, or not associate with one another destroys the opportunity to make connections and understand people from different diversified backgrounds. Mentally isolating oneself from society and labeling those that don't follow a certain belief system as lost or condemned is simply untrue. Religious belief does not determine if a person is good or not. Everyone has something good to offer to this world no matter where they were born or what they believe in.

At some point in our existence, collaboration has to be the focal point on survival and preservation of all good ideals and cultures. Our diversity is part of our holistic history. Our origins have many different theories and claims, but no one can argue that existing at all is nothing short of a miracle. The world has been through so many changes. We have faced so many different challenges overcoming feats of hardship and survival and still we stand today. We now have new challenges that have been brought on by rapid modernization of the planet. Most of our problems are economic, but this is only because our goals are advancement in profit instead of advancement of people.

In some religions and cultures around the world, women do not have the rights and privileges that they have been granted in most of the western world. There is no justification to ever lessen someone's importance based off of gender or race or religion. There is also no justification to try and control the rights or privileges of a certain group. There are a lot of different examples of this, especially when it comes to race, gender, and sexual orientation. In a perfect world every group should have the same rights as the next. This should not be left up to politics or religious views, but it is used this way to keep a false control on viewpoints.

Most religions teach a message of love and acceptance for your fellow man. The sad thing is people misuse religion to try and justify why we shouldn't love and accept one another. Too often people of different religions or even agnostics and atheists are labeled. If someone chooses not to follow any faith or believe in a deity, then that does not make them a bad person. If they commit no crimes and break no laws, then technically they are just as good as a person as anyone else regardless of belief.

One thing that cannot be argued is that we came from something. Scientific evidence proves that there is a possibility of some type of evolutionary background to our species, which is Homo sapiens. None of us have hard-nose facts that are completely tangibly evident; otherwise, there would be no argument about the truth of our beginning. Our energy and focus needs to be on living. None of us asked to exist. We are all here with the same wants and needs. We are curious and vulnerable. We need to focus on each other and the betterment of society and the world instead of worrying about beliefs and things that separate us.

According to an article written in October of 2010 by "CNN," Sunday mornings in America are the most segregated day of the week. The racial lines don't cross between churches, and most people of worship overwhelmingly only worship with their own race or demographic. This is a very interesting fact. Even at a time of worship there is an obvious segregation that not even religion has been able to fix. But is religion supposed to fix this? Or are we as people supposed to confront this and fix it? Too often religion is used as a form of segregation instead of bringing people together.

In the midst of tragedy and hardship we come together for the common goal of survival. Someday in the midst of segregation of faiths we will come together for the most powerful thing in the world: love. A love that sees through race, religion, and culture is inside of us all. Good intentions are a natural part of us just as evil is. Because of circumstances that lead to selfish endeavors we forget about our hearts. There are scientific studies that suggest that love affects our health and immune systems. If any of it is true, could it be possible that low self-esteem, obesity, and numerous other health issues that we suffer from are a result of a lack of love in society?

Outside of religion, loving one another isn't dynamically popular because of our every man for himself mentality. Getting support outside of one's family or group is really rare. Most of the time people only support each other when there is mutual benefit. Although having mutual benefit is great, we have put a dollar value on our time and efforts. We can see our way out of this by a changing the way we value each other.

I believe people don't understand what religion was meant to be. Religion is simply a tool for those that believe in life after death. It is meant to direct a type of moral compass while living. It was not meant to be used as an excuse for violence or hatred. It seems that the byproduct of most religions is to eat away at our humanity. Although this is my own personal opinion, it is not meant to offend anyone that believes differently. I will always respect religion and different cultures. But I will always draw the line at the use of religion for dubious acts and thinking. We are better than that.

Although I do not follow any religions, I have grown to have the most respect for the Baha'i Faith. Their teachings encourage the Unity of all Religions and the Unity of Humanity. This is exactly what the world needs for collective prosperity. In this mortal life we all face the same fate. That fate is to one day die. What we do with our lives is not only important to us as individuals but it is even more important for all of us. Not just for our family and friends. All of us have a part in history, and if we make a big enough impact on the world in a positive way then we never really die. An idea or ideal can live on forever through the people that we influence throughout our lives. We all have the ability to change the world this way. Every single one of us is connected this way.

One of the biggest enemies to peace and unity is religious extremism. Almost every religion has a group of extremists that try their best to start trouble and preach a message of division and hatred. Westboro Baptist Church is probably one of the best-known groups in the United States to do this. They openly preach a message that slanders military members and veterans. They protest and praise the deaths of military veterans during funerals. This is absolutely distasteful and evil. Westboro Baptist Church is the exact opposite of what most religious churches represent.

Going even further with religious extremism are Muslim terrorists. As a result of terrorism, Islam has been targeted with a lot of discrimination and social unacceptance. This is completely unfair and not logical. The name of this group of people should be simply Terrorists. I believe disconnecting the Muslim part is a very important distinction. Not all Muslims are terrorists or are at risk of becoming terrorists. They are exactly the opposite; a peaceful and loving culture that values very similar things as most other religions. When we are met with hatred we should get in the habit of having a loving response. Dr. Martin Luther King would have been a champion of peace in the times that we face today. He once said, "Darkness cannot drive out darkness; only light can do that. Hate cannot drive out hate; only love can do that." These words are true to life, and instead of speaking it or admiring the wisdom of Dr. Martin Luther King we should all live this way.

Instead of living in acceptance we are all guilty of judging each other and figuring out ways to justify discrimination. We try to justify discrimination with our religion or ideals. Recently the gay community was targeted by Christian fundamentalists. There was an anti-gay bill that was trying to be passed in Arizona. In the bill store owners, restaurant owners, and businesses would be given the right to choose not to give services to gay people if they chose to do so. This is discrimination and no different than Black people not being allowed to go into certain public places back in the early to mid 1900s. Gay marriage and gay rights has been a major touching point lately in all aspects of culture. Don't they deserve to live the way they choose to as long as they cause no harm to anyone else? Isn't it ethically wrong to tell someone how they have to live outside of the laws of the land? There is no freedom if gay people are not allowed to be who they are.

The First Amendment to the United States Constitution says that "Congress shall make no law respecting an establishment of religion, or prohibiting the free exercise thereof." Attempting to pass laws giving religions people the ability to do anything to non-religious people violates the separation of church and state. The First Amendment was established to avoid things like this. To make sure that every man or woman or organization is treated equal in the eyes of government with no favoritism. Why is there such an urge for religious people to try and control how other people live their lives?

They are free to make suggestions, but ultimately it is up to the individual how they choose to live their life. We are not even sure if people choose to be gay and this is a big debate. If they are born gay then it really does not fall under the umbrella of free will.

In 2011 the United Nations Human Rights Council passed one of the first resolutions recognizing the LGBT rights. LGBT stands for Lesbian, Gay, Bisexual and Transgender. A lot of religions condemn the LGBT community. In some countries they are executed, tortured, and Imprisoned. This is exactly why there was a human rights issue with the way these normal, loving people were being treated.

In some countries being gay or LGBT is punishable by life in prison and sometimes even the death penalty. Recently Ugandan President Yoweri Museveni signed into law a bill that toughens penalties against gay people. He thinks that most homosexual acts are crimes punishable by life in prison. The United States Government suggested that he not pass this bill which is very discriminatory but he did not listen and passed it anyway. This could potentially be a human rights violation, according to the United Nations Human Rights Council. President Yoweri Museveni of Uganda says that he is very disappointed with the United States and the way that we conduct ourselves when it comes to gay rights. The new law also proposes years in prison for anyone who counsels or reaches out to gays and lesbians. The purpose of the bill is to isolate and punish gays and lesbians as much as possible. Anyone that is gay or lesbian will most definitely keep it private for fear of their freedom and safety. As you can see there is a long way to go in the terms of acceptance for the LGBT community. Homosexuality is illegal in 38 African countries. They believe that if there are not tough punishments for the gay community then it will destroy the traditional family unit of Man and Woman. The true pursuit of happiness in life should not involve making the lives of other people miserable. There is nothing to gain in causing misery and injustice. Maybe in the near future our minds will evolve and we will accept the diversity of Human Beings and truly appreciate our differences instead of condemning what we do not understand. In a lot of situations we would do better by listening to our hearts and realizing that there is nothing to gain in discrimination.

Some people believe that if there was no religion at all then the world would be a better place. But that is not true. We would just find other ways to fight or hate each other. Religion has been the major reason for a lot of morals and structure in all societies around the world. Just because someone doesn't follow any religion does not mean that they are damned or lack a moral compass. Love and respect are not limited to religious belief systems. If there is a god then he created every single person on this planet and is represented somehow in every culture of the world.

We should be very worried about society if it continues on this path. We took prayer out of schools in America because of religious freedom issues. Should we really care so much if our children learn to pray in school regardless of what religion it is? Prayer gives a sense of unity and comfort. It also crosses a lot of cultural boundaries. There should be freedom of religion in all schools because It creates a bridge of understanding. Even if you do not believe in a particular religion it is still productive to understand its customs and history. We have to be more connected than we are. There is great ignorance in dismissing anyone's traditions or beliefs. Whether it is real or fake should not be part of the concern. The concern should be unity and prosperity, not segregation connected with non-productive opinions.

Although we all have the right to our own opinions, everyone has the right to a happy life full of joy, happiness, and equality. One day through the realization of our own faults we will re-connect with our fellow man...

WAR AND CONSEQUENCE

War has been the resolution to opposing powers and countries since the dawn of civilization. War has evolved tremendously over the years. New technology creates new ways of fighting wars. We are able to send drones to take care of business without risking lives in surveillance missions. The weapons and technology have evolved, but the reasons we fight one another hasn't. Does it really matter how advanced our technology is, or how many accomplishments we make if our way of thinking and resolving conflict doesn't evolve also? The consequences of war are much deeper than who wins, or who loses. It is deeper than the lives lost or the sacrifices that were made by whoever is fighting. The choice to wage war is based off of the intent for revenge, justice, or hatred.

Is the true definition of honor or justice worthy of being connected with war? In war, lives are taken. Whether those lives are good or bad does not matter when we are all capable of the same things that we oppose or disagree with. War has become a solution to our problems and differences that our world has outgrown. Too many lives are affected by its consequences. The effects are psychological and also deceive the future. When we as humans disagree with one another and there seems to be no common ground met on the issue then it has the possibility to lead to conflict. Conflict can be as simple as clashing ideas that could possibly lead to people getting hurt when it is on the scale of powerful opposing countries.

We have let the power to wage war or fight cloud the decisions of what motivates us. Power is not meant to be wielded or demonstrated. Power is meant to be distributed. The world is short on those that want to distribute power rather than use it. Our willingness to use war to solve problems leaves a psychological impression of false solution. When attacked, the response is to retaliate with bigger force or continue to fight with no meaning. We call this resolve. The goal is to win but there is no true winner. We all lose because we lowered ourselves to the same psychological resolutions of those men in primitive tribes at the dawn of civilization. Someday the power of choosing not to partake in war will set the tone in our future.

The consequence of fighting and killing each other tells us that it is ok to do this if we are attacked or threatened. This continuation of war sets the tone for the psychological decisions of future generations. There has to be change in the favor of better alternatives to solving conflicts. Naturally there is a need to respond to a country that attacks your own. But we are not in the early years of civilization or the middle ages. What would happen if a country got attacked and didn't respond with war? What if there was a refusal to participate in senseless killing? Wouldn't this type of restraint be more powerful than any vengeful response or weapon? The consequence of not responding with violence but expressing the condemnation of the attack would send a bigger message than that of war or military response.

Leadership has to lead by example and there has to be

an evolution in the way that we do things for the betterment of our collective futures. The consequence of not taking care of this responsibility is a big reason why we still fight wars today. Fear is a big factor of why things stay the same. Promoting power around the world long enough regardless of how powerful you are will eventually become less feared and more of an act of oppression. When people feel oppressed they eventually rise up or rebel, or they fight just for the simple reason of resistance. In some cases this can be related to terrorism or random acts of violence in the middle-east and around the world.

War also has astounding effects on human behavior. War has popularized video game genres for years. Kids and young adults play very realistic war-torn video games every day. Should we as a society wonder if these video games play any role in desensitizing our youth or future generations? The less one values the life of his fellow man the possibility of violent response to conflict is much higher. We as a society are exposed to too much violence. If we compare violent movies of today to the ones in the past we have obviously become more and more violent and gruesome in our expression of action. It is not rare to see people's limbs or heads being blown off in every action film these days.

With gun violence, one of the main focal points these days, an obvious observation tells us that the blame cannot be placed only on the guns or how easily they are accessed. It is very irresponsible to blame an object or a weapon for violence because it has no power without the person. But that is exactly what we do. When a school shooting happens or violence is on the rise we blame the weapons as if the people had no control of committing these violent acts and the weapons made them do it. We have to ask the hard questions and look deeper to get the answers that we need to solve the issue of violence. We have to take responsibility as a society for the violence that is such a normal part of the culture that we have created.

We have to evaluate our culture and what fuels and influences the violence. It cannot be blamed on one thing; it is a synergy of a great multitude of things that has affected the way that we think and how we act. If there were no violent video games or movies, would people be so accepting of violence and committing violent acts? If there was less violence in the world and less war, would that influence people to think more constructively in terms of creating new tools of war? Everything that we do is connected. Every decision made on a big enough scale will affect everyone. You can see how everything affects us very easily if you open your eyes and focus. For example, how many more violent video games had plots that were centered towards terrorism after September 11th? Or how many more action movies had plots centered towards terrorism, or bombings after September 11th? Also, how much do media outlets speak of "possible" terrorism that has not even happened yet? They speak of possible scenarios that are completely hypothetical which can very possibly influence someone to do it or give a terrorist new ideas.

One event in human history has so much influence that it breaches its way into our normal everyday lives and also into our culture. How many more things have snuck into our lives masked as something else while it slowly deteriorates our love and value for one another? It sneaks in veiled as entertainment, but it is much deeper. We have to be careful of these things and make sure that we keep our values in order and not be programmed by the sensations of entertainment that was influenced by a sacred tragedy.

There is a war going on that doesn't involved weapons or violence. This war is inside of all of us. It is a war on our morals and emotions. It is masked into our daily lives and is subtle and unrecognizable because it has become a socially acceptable normality. It has its grips on our minds and is a driving force of new ideas that will make things worse. The only way to fix it is to recognize what it is and what it does and not allow it to influence our outlook on life in any type of way. We must also not allow it to change our value for life. We must desperately hold on to our genuine care for our fellow man. Anger, Greed, Pride, and Superiority must be thrown to the side. We are one World.

For centuries we have been fighting wars of survival and disagreement against each other. It is time that we lay down our petty differences and fight against things that pose a bigger threat to our survival. Nonviolence is the only true way to defeat an enemy. As time passes and technology advances through new discoveries and disciplines, our minds should advance in the way that we solve conflicts. But the reality is that our thinking does not evolve. We just get better at killing each other.

Whether war is justified or not, no one ever questions the impact it will have on the innocent people caught in between. The website www.iraqbodycount.org shows over 120,000 civilians have been killed in Iraq since the invasion in the year 2003. That is a huge number, and it keeps growing higher every day even though the war in Iraq is over. This is a direct result of the consequences of our invasion that was fueled by the terrorist attacks on September 11th, 2001. In the September 11th attacks roughly 3,000 innocent Americans were killed. Are 3,000 American lives equal to 120,000 or more Iraqi lives?

We have caused a significant amount of damage just in Iraq, and that is much higher than the damage caused on September 11th. But this isn't damage done to our enemies.

This is damage done to innocent people that had arguably had no intentions on harming U.S. citizens or even their own people. We have to think about the consequences of our decision to go into Iraq. We caused much more harm than good. Would it be fair to think that our actions in Iraq would help fuel more terrorism? Would it cause resentment and more hatred towards the United States? The answer is an obvious yes.

Bradley Manning, who served as an Army Intelligence Analyst, leaked classified information about the Iraq and Afghanistan Wars. He claimed that the United States military committed war crimes and tried to cover it up. He was charged with aiding the enemy and sentenced to 20 years in prison. Through an organization called WikiLeaks he released files and video of the U.S. Military killing suspected terrorists that later turned out to be members of the media and innocent people. There were no consequences for the parties involved.

Although the above is only one instance of a technical war crime, where should we draw the line? It should be acknowledged that there is great possibility for human error when it comes to fighting wars. Shouldn't this be enough deterrence for us to choose not to go to war? How much are American lives worth compared to the lives of people that reside in other countries? The actions of our military demonstrate that American lives seem to be more important since we have killed far more civilians oversees than terrorism has in America. The consequences go much deeper than just deaths of innocents. Exposing undeveloped countries to uncharted violence and killing has to have a negative effect on their world view and psychological development.

If violence and killing become normal, then wouldn't it be likely that they take on the traits of what they witness? We have created a breeding ground for terrorism in a never-ending cycle of war. Was this the goal all along? Since our troops left Iraq they have continued to fight amongst themselves. There are thousands of deaths recorded because of how unstable we left Iraq. These deaths can also be blamed on our decision to invade Iraq. After September 11th Americans wanted justice. But justice can come in many forms. The type of justice that we sought out was not planned well and also a big mistake. We will pay for this mistake possibly for many generations. The Iraqi people will also pay for our mistakes.

The history of American wars and conflicts has a horribly high death toll. In World War 2 American bombers dropped atomic bombs on 2 Japanese locations. They were Hiroshima and Nagasaki. On August 9th, 1945, the Island of Nagasaki, Japan, was bombed. The atomic blast killed 32% of the population there. By December of 1945 it is estimated that 60,000 to 90,000 people had been killed as a result of the atomic bomb and its after effects of radiation poisoning on the population.

Three days before Nagasaki was bombed Hiroshima was bombed also. The atomic blast killed 45,000 people the first day. 19,000 more people died in the following 4 months as a result of radiation poison and sickness from radiation. Hundreds of survivors were expected to die from cancers and other complications during the next 30 years after the atomic bomb was dropped. With the death toll so high in Japan and the horrific after-effects, it is hard to imagine how the Japanese people survived morally through what could be compared to an Apocalypse.

The total death count in World War 2, which lasted from September of 1939 to September of 1945, is phenomenal. World War 2 was the deadliest military conflict in history. It is estimated that over 80 million people were killed. That was almost 3% of the world population. The most astonishing number is the amount of civilians killed, which totaled somewhere between 40 and 50 million. Another 15 to 20 million died from war-related famine and diseases. Up to 25 million military personnel were killed and almost 5 million prisoners of war suffered the same fate. It is very interesting that after such a horrific war and death toll that any human being on this planet would ever consider going to war again. But as history shows we as a collective do not really learn from the past. Instead we keep on repeating the same things over and over again, but just in a different way. It is very interesting that we would not try to find better ways of solving problems when it comes to wars of conflict.

Moving on in history to the Korean War, there are even more horrible death tolls. The Korean War began in June of 1950 and ended in July of 1953 as a result of Kim Il-Sung wanting to reunify North and South Korea. According to the Department of Defense, The United States suffered over 30,000 battle deaths and almost 3,000 non-battle deaths. It is believed that over 8,000 people went missing in action and never found. That is a very sad number. South Korea suffered almost 400,000 civilian casualties and close to 138,000 military deaths. The PVA (Peoples Volunteer Army) of China also had about 400,000 casualties and almost 500,000 wounded. North Korea's Volunteer Army suffered over 100,000 war-related deaths, over 300,000 wounded, and over 30,000 non-war-related casualties. North Korea's Volunteer Army also lost over 7,000 personnel and deemed them missing in action. About 20,000 soldiers were also captured.

Next up was the Vietnam War that began with the Communist Democratic Republic of Vietnam and its allies against the United States–supported Republic of Vietnam, which is South Vietnam. The Vietnam War lasted from 1959 to April 30th, 1975. The Vietnam War was also known as the second Indochina War and the Vietnam Conflict, or the American War in as per Vietnam natives. The Soviet Union and China were supporters of the Communist North Vietnam, and United States and its allies supported South Vietnam, which was anti-Communist. The Vietnam War was one of the longest and casualty-stricken wars of the 1900s. We still see the effects of this war on American Military Veterans in the United States from chemical exposures like Agent Orange and soldiers with missing limbs.

The popularity of the Vietnam War with the American public was not very high. Veterans came home after the war ashamed of themselves and also the country. People would spit on soldiers and publicly show their disapproval and unhappiness with our country being involved in Vietnam. It was a bad time in America for veterans returning from the war because of the social bias and also the lack of support given to veterans. There are many horror stories about the Vietnam War. There were not many positive things about it in the media and also the eyes of the world that watched it all unfold.

Estimates of casualties for the Vietnam War suggest that up to 4 million people died over the course of conflict. It is also estimated that upwards of 400,000 South Vietnamese civilians were killed. Over 60,000 North Vietnamese civilians died as a result of campaigns carried out by the South and its allies. The official U.S. Department of Defense figure suggests that upwards of 1.1 million people were killed in Vietnam from 1965 to 1974. But the Defense Department believes that the official number of casualties needs to be deflated by 30% of the original estimate.

What are the results of our heavy history of wars and conflict? Do you believe that there are consequences that last for generations? Hearing the news reporting numbers of thousands of people dead or even millions has become a social normality. Violence is so acceptable that almost anyone is willing to resort to it in situations of conflict. Has our war-torn culture lead us down a path of eventual destruction through war? Dropping bombs or getting involved militarily as a country has become so easy that we bear on with the conflicts of the present day. We have been in Afghanistan for 13 years. Is it truly productive or is it a cash cow for corporate contractors that don't want lose their profits?

The consequences of war reach far beyond its effects on veterans. It has become too much of a norm in society that war is part of politics as if the lives involved are simply pawns or chess board pieces. The amount of money that our government spends on research for new and more efficient wars of killing each other is a bad example, not only to our country but to the rest of the world. When the United States used the first atomic bomb it was believed that it would be a weapon that would keep peace in the world. But all it did was create desire for the atomic bomb by other countries. It became a symbol of power to possess it instead of a symbol of peace.

It is obvious that our wars of the past have a great influence on our present wars and wars of the future. One thing that holds true is that it seems that we don't learn much from fighting wars. So many countries today are on the brink of all-out war and civil unrest that it makes you wonder if we will ever change. Will there ever be real peace in the world? There will never be peace in the world until a major country sets an example of peace. There has to be a major event that would normally not result in a peaceful outcome to set an example. We are leaders and also followers but deep down everyone wants to follow good examples that have been lined out for them. We have to choose to refrain from all types of violence and talk out our problems instead of jumping to the guns and military options. Military resources are overused in all sorts of situations. Overuse of military resources weakens a country's economy and also sets a bad example for future leadership.

We have to acknowledge our mistakes and learn from them. We have to refuse to make the same mistakes over and over again. The consequences of not going through this process is exactly why we are in the conflicts and situations we are today with terrorism and domestic threats. Although terrorism has killed many innocent people in the military and United States due to the September 11th attacks, we have killed more foreign civilians with our presence in Iraq and Afghanistan. We have to ask ourselves, is it worth it to keep doing what we are doing or is there another way? We are responsible for our actions and choices. Are our actions and choices of today better for our future?

Someday we might learn that choosing to go to war solves nothing. Hatred breeds more hatred, and revenge breeds more revenge. A never-ending cycle fixes nothing at all. The consequences make peace truly impossible. Peace should be the end goal. War can never be involved in a peaceful outcome. You might kill an enemy or stop him temporarily, but eventually that enemy will come back in a different form to fight once again. There are no true winners in war. Everyone wins when the road to non-violence and diplomatic solutions is taken. With enough influence and enlightenment, peace will prevail. We just have to give it the chance that it has always deserved. A peaceful world starts with our hearts. We have always had the power to wage peace. I think it is about time that we used our power just for that….

THE MISUSE OF POWER

THE MISUSE AND ABUSE OF POWER HAS ALWAYS BEEN a benefit of being in control. Since the ages of kings and kingdoms there are stories of corruption, secret alliances, and greed. It still holds true today in a different time. It is easy to see that power corrupts those that have it. Most don't completely go to the dark side and become evil, but they fall in love and get comfortable with the pedestal of importance. To be seduced by power in some way is almost a natural occurrence. Power grants the possessor many options, whether influential or political. Power can also be the downfall of a person when taken too far. History has shown us many examples of this.

To overcome the seductiveness of power one has to have a completely selfless mindset. The mental capacity of selflessness has many degrees. Simply thinking about other people does not equate to selflessness if nothing is executed to validate your thoughts or intentions. The absence of action would leave the idea of selflessness somewhere in the realm of intention. Power was never meant to be harnessed by a small group or individuals. Power is meant to be distributed so that it recycles and uplifts weak links tied to the collective.

The misuse of power doesn't just pertain to someone abusing it. It also pertains to those that do not use it at all. A good example of this is our struggling economy. There are many companies in the world that are worth billions and billions of dollars. There are also individuals that are worth billions. These entities are what should be classified as stagnant and only represent the title of profit victory. Profit is a financial achievement that every company and every person seeks. This makes profit the goal. After the goal of profit is secured, then businesses naturally expand and maybe purchase or buy out competitors.

When a company or corporation buys out a competitor or merges with one it isn't a bad thing but it eliminates competition. When competition is eliminated then jobs are lost, which leaves those unlucky individuals looking for new sources of income and searching for a new employer. These juggernaut companies do nothing for the economy other than bleed as much profit as possible. They don't plant any seeds in the economy that lead to growth in other sectors of our monetary system. The mission is to do what benefits the profit or workings of the company. What would be the effect if these juggernaut companies floated their excess billions to startup companies in completely different industries rather than sit on this money collecting meaningless interest and dividends?

Inherently, this approach to economic growth would be perfect. Businesses close down and go away all the time, but those companies at the top have to pitch a hand in recreating new business. They have the power to move and influence economic trends and control, but they only use their power for self-expansion and profit. This is where the connection is lost. The realization of the power they have overshadows their worth. This basic knowledge executed needs no government intervention when it comes to boosting the economy because by default the top tier billion dollar companies would be planting seeds that grow, and that growth could possibly lead to even more seeds being planted and jobs being created. This goes hand in hand with the phrase that says the "Rich Get Richer" because it is completely true.

There are no limits to how big a company or corporation can grow but is it really a good idea economically? Is it a good idea to grow a corporation so big and powerful that if it fails, then it will have devastating effects on the entire world economy? Logistical recovery from failure almost becomes impossible if a big corporation or bank fails. One example is HSBC Bank. HSBC bank was under investigation for laundering money for drug cartels and possible ties to terrorist groups. The executives knowingly did this but served no prison time because it would have had negative implications for the global economy. Their punishment was simply a fine.

These crimes involved millions and millions of dollars with evidence and proof directly tied to the guilty parties, and because they are bank executives of a very large bank they don't have to serve any time in prison. This doesn't compare very well to the normal citizen. Bank robbers for theft of more than 200,000 dollars can serve up to a maximum of 3 life sentences in prison. The comparison makes no sense at all, does it? This is one of the biggest indications that there are 2 judicial systems at work here. For normal people that break laws they are punished to the full extent of the law and the crime. But if you are very powerful and putting you behind bars affects the economy, then you are immune to prison time for crime.

This type of injustice should not be tolerated but it goes on and on, and is a result of banks and corporations becoming too big and too powerful. We have to ask ourselves hard questions moving forward in society. It seems like the best benefit of being a bank executive or corporation executive is immunity to broken laws if your conviction will negatively impact the economy. This is a prime example of what misuse of power is.

Is it possible that people get addicted to money? There is a saying that the rich get richer. Could money and power be some kind of void that people use to fill in the gaps in their lives? Just like drugs or sex or alcohol it could eventually be the downfall of a person. On a bigger scale the richest of the rich that directly affect the economy can lead us to a similar downfall.

Power corrupts because most people don't have the capacity to do something positive and selfless once they acquire power. It's really sad to stop and look around and realize that almost everyone wants some kind of power. Something in society makes us feel small. Our selfishness has created the mentality that will eventually be the downfall of our economy and possibly even our nation if we don't wake up. Power is so seductive that people lose their connection to humanity and only care about themselves.

Sadly our Federal Government grossly abuses power to intimidate its citizens. One of the biggest examples of this recently was with Aaron Hillel Swartz. Aaron Hillel Swartz was a computer programmer, internet activist, writer, and also a political organizer. Aaron was involved in the development of RSS web feed format and the organizer of Creative Commons. He also wrote the framework for the social news site Reddit. He eventually became a partner after Reddit merged with his company called Infogami.

Aaron Swartz was involved in a lot of social and civic awareness activism. He also helped launch the Progressive Change Campaign Committee in 2009 to help learn more about online activism. He was a research fellow at Harvard's Lab on Institutional Corruption under the direct of Lawrence

Lessig. Aaron Swartz was a very passionate person when it came to rules and freedoms regarding the subjects of information and the internet. In January of 2011 he was arrest by M.I.T. Police for breaking and entering. He downloaded academic journal articles from an academic library called JSTOR. Aaron was charged with two counts of wire fraud and 11 violations of the computer fraud and abuse act. The maximum penalty would be 1 million dollars in fines and 35 years in prison if convicted.

Aaron spent 2 years fighting the charges and used up all of the money that he had accumulated because of his success. His lawyers offered plea bargains and the federal prosecutors denied all of them. They were dead set on charging him with the maximum penalty even though JSTOR dropped all charges of violating their terms agreement. This is an example of the government overstepping on civil cases between a company and its users. Things like this should not be allowed or tolerated in a free society. But it seems like it is wishful thinking. Fairness has evolved into power and intimidation.

Aaron Swartz committed suicide after the prosecution denied his second offer of a plea bargain. He was 26 years old. It is a very sad story of power and bullying going so far out of control that is causes someone to end their own life. What was the goal of it all? There are no lessons to be learned. Only ugliness and unnecessary tragedy was the result. His supposed crimes were too minor in comparison to other major crimes. Did you know that assaulting a Supreme Court Justice can get you up to only 1 year in prison, and assaulting a Supreme Court Justice with a dangerous weapon could get you up to 10 years in prison? You would think that these 2 types of crimes are much more severe than downloading academic papers from an online school publishing library.

If you threaten the President of the United States you can

get up to 5 years in prison. If you knowingly spread AIDS you can face a maximum of 10 years in prison. If you sell child pornography you could get up to 20 years in prison. For armed bank robbery you can get up to 25 years in prison. Helping terrorists develop a nuclear weapon could get you up to 20 years in prison. Aaron Swartz downloaded Academic papers from JSTOR and was facing up to 50 years in prison. He was not hacking nor doing anything illegal but he would get more prison time than real criminals that actually do harm to others or threaten national security because of the overreaching disgusting power trip that our government is currently drunken with.

HSBC Bank executives committed wire fraud with the largest drug cartels and terrorists in the world but served no prison time. There seems to be a lot of comfort in breaking the law when you have power. Power is dangerous because it is often in the wrong hands. It is misused to fit certain agendas that have nothing to do with progressiveness. Power seems to only serve the individuals that have it. They use the power that they have to gain even more power.

One of the biggest misuses of power is the catastrophic divide of income inequality. In 2014 the richest 85 people have more money than the poorest 3 and a half billion people in the world. The wealthiest people in the world hide their money in foreign and secret bank accounts to avoid taxes and penalties. Their greed had gotten so out of control that they don't realize the damage they are doing to the world economy. Hoarding money does not support the capitalist structure. Who is going to be able to buy products from the richest companies in the world if half of the world cannot even afford their products? They don't realize that recycling their wealth so that it trickles down into society in the form of grants, benefits, and opportunities makes the whole system of capitalism stronger. These people don't care about the system. As poverty gets worse and worse, they continue to only care about their own obscene levels of wealth and power. For some people money became an addiction for them. Just like drug addicts they need more and more. Since the late 1970s, tax rates for the richest people in the world have fallen in 29 of the 30 countries for which data is available. Wealthy people and companies hide over 21 trillion in wealth in a web of tax havens around the world. In the United States 95% of the top 1% captured over 90% of the financial growth after the 2009 financial crisis. Sadly this was a crisis caused by them and they are the ones that benefited the most from it.

In the United States even the presidential elections are controlled by the most rich and powerful people in the country. There are 2 different elections that take place for which a president is decided upon. The first election is the money election. It is an election that is run by the top funders of elections in the United States. The funders get to pick the candidate that best aligns with their goals and agendas. These funders are about 0.5% of the United States population. This means there are only about 100 thousand people that control this part of the election. The second election is called the general election, where the people get to choose the candidates, but only after the funders have chosen the candidates that will run for president.

This leads to a false illusion of choice because regardless of which person they vote for, Democrat or Republican, the funders have already chosen 1 of each that both suit the needs of their power and agenda. The vast majority of the funders only want to look out for themselves and the benefits of their power. This is for private interest and not public interest. This is an absolute corruption. This is not a corruption that breaks the law. This is a corruption that is perfectly legal. Congress has evolved into a dependency on the funders.

In this system the members are dependent on the tiniest fraction of people for their election. This means that the tiniest number of people can block any kind of reform. People go about their lives while this manipulation of power and misuse of government goes on. They choose not to think too deeply about many things and get attached to wedge issues that are implanted in their minds during the political season. It is a combination of a lot of things. With the recovery of the economy and issues surrounding health benefits, who has time to think about the fairness of government? It is very distracting to be part of any political party.

We need a government that works. Not one that works for the left or the right, but for everyone in the United States. We can never have any sensible reform with a system in place like this. There will never be real or fair elections in a system in place like this. The only way to fix this problem is for the funder influence to be spread among the people of America instead of only the richest people in America being the funders. To do this only requires a statute that regulates campaigns to citizen-funded only campaigns. Sadly, a lot of change doesn't happen because of hopelessness. The United States is not a republic that is dependent on the people. If it is not dependent on the citizens, then are those citizens really free and is this really a democracy? Currently the evidence shows that the United States is simply a corporation that only imitates freedom.

In 2013 Edward Snowden, a former Booz-Allen contractor exposed that the government was recording every phone call, text message, and email of every American citizen. As a result of leaking this information, Edward Snowden was charged with espionage. Espionage is an individual that obtained secret or confidential information without permission. This spy program was one of the most secret programs in United States Government. These spy programs were controlled by the National Security Agency. This is a big abuse of power by government, but some people don't think what Edward Snowden did was right. They believe that he should have never said anything. Opinions don't overshadow facts. There is no reason that the government needs to record everyone's phone calls or track everyone's emails. The real problem is logic.

The government claims that they are not using information against normal law-abiding citizens and are only doing this type of spying to collect data on potential national security threats such as terrorists. Recording everyone's information is really the only way to track potential terrorist threats. There is no real way to demographically track a threat that is unknown with no leads. Collecting data and meta-data on everyone gives the N.S.A. the ability to filter data. They can track everything from emails from potentially threatening countries to key word phrases spoken on a telephone. After the data is collected it can be investigated and sorted. The program that controlled all of this was called PRISM.

PRISM is a mass electronic surveillance program that was launched in 2007 by the National Security Agency in partnership with the British Government. The PRISM program was started by the Bush Administration under the Protect America Act. The PRISM program collects internet communications based of demands made by internet companies such as Google and even Apple under section 702 of the Foreign Intelligence Act in the year 2008. At first it was only going to be a tool used to turn over any data that matched court approved search terms. But power can be abused and misused all too easily. There are stories of government officials with access to this power using it to spy on politicians, family members, and even famous actors. We have to draw the line somewhere and figure out what the consequences are moving forward.

This would not be necessary if the U.S. Government had not created so many foreign enemies over the years. Now we are forced to increase security and spend billions and billions more each year on national security. The abuse of power and government has gotten so out of control that now the government has no choice but to use the power given to them on their own citizens. This is simply a lack of true leadership. Leadership should be in the business of granting power instead of increasing its own power. Increasing power only leads to the misuse and abuse of it. I hope that someday we realize the mistakes we have made and change course to a much brighter future. The Government of the United States has lost the connection to its citizens in favor of alliances driven by greed.

POLITICS AND WEDGE ISSUES

A WEDGE ISSUE IS A SOCIAL OR POLITICAL ISSUE, and it is often used in a controversial nature to distract or ignite strong emotions or even moral reactions to many types of social political subjects. An example of a wedge issue is gay marriage. Most people believe that gay marriage is not right because the Bible says that marriage is supposed to be between a man and a woman. This touches on many different religious beliefs alongside Christianity. But would this fall under the category of forcing one's belief on another? The diversity of moral thought is never considered, and this ignites issues such as gay marriage. If 2 men or 2 women choose to get married, wouldn't it fall under the category of freedom or free will instead of religion? There has to be a line drawn somewhere so that religious beliefs aren't forced on someone else's chosen lifestyle.

Another purpose of wedge issues is to distract us from legislation or laws being passed that we may not completely agree with. Wedge issues also turn our attention away from very serious world events. The media reports the news but constantly searches for "new" subject matters and controversy to report. This in turn could have negative impacts on things that we should all be paying attention to in great detail. Wedge issues are a distraction from the sustainability of our culture and society. The real issues like energy consumption, national debt, science and research funding, are all lost under the weight of issues that hold no bearing on our collective advancement and growth. Gay people being married or interracial issues have nothing to do with advancement in civilization, but these kinds of issues get front coverage news reports before anything else. Some may argue that these issues are valid social issues that should be left for debate but it is time for us to move on.

The same issues have been talked about and debated on for many years now. Each new election is just a different guy talking about the same issues we have been having for years but in a different order. Nothing has really changed, and it is because our culture has not changed. In Every election taxes are talked about, immigration is touched on, and also national security. People want lower taxes or tax cuts. The only reason taxes are constantly a subject is because of growing national debt. If taxes were the solution to paying off the debt then our country would have never gotten this far down the debt path. The real issue is uncontrolled government spending. There aren't enough things to be taxed to pay off the debt, but no politician is going to say that in an election, because that is not what people want to hear. The reality of our problems is danced around instead of faced. Instead of solving problems we collectively push them to the side as long as our emotional connections are satisfied.

There aren't many strong minds that discredit this form of "thought" segregation. The ability to embrace everything that should tear us apart seems rare these days. Immigration has always been one of those wedge issues where no one can really find a common ground on how to deal with it. Technically all of us are immigrants. Part of the American dream is to have safe schools and neighborhoods for our children and the chance to advance ourselves and our families. Does anyone ever think that it's not just Americans that want this? The opportunities that we have in America are very attractive to foreigners and even more attractive if they are trying to escape a violent country with fewer rights and no opportunities. Part of the problem is that we are not sympathetic to the situations of others, and this causes a lot of confusion as to why someone would want to take the risk of coming to America Illegally.

Our connection with the wedge issue of immigration is lost because we think of ourselves as higher beings of existence and that there is some type of difference between us and immigrants other than where we were born. This way of thinking is a byproduct of another wedge issue that America has had for years now, and that is Race. Politicians use a lot of tactics to win over certain racial votes. But why shouldn't they? We still live in a day in age where race is still a touchy subject. Hate crimes are still a common thing and openly racial segregated places still exist. A lot of politicians come with a message of equality and try to cater to whichever targeted demographic with some type of promised benefits or favoritism that is motivated by politically driven sympathy. It may seem like this form of politics is dirty, but these politicians are just playing off of the emotions and viewpoints of the people. We are the guilty ones because, we give power to these racially charged subjects and we allow politicians to use it against us and divide us even more. Politics is the exact opposite of unity because of how politicians use it against the people that they claim to want to bring together.

These wedge issues are put in the form of propositions and ballad initiatives to attract voters and lure them into voting only based on the subject matter of these issues. It's a perfect example of divide and conquer, because people think with their emotions and overlook the fact that they may be losing their jobs, their homes, or even their rights. Most people don't do much research about their candidates because they have already chosen which side they are on. Republicans and Democrats have had a lot of different changes in their parties over the years that would most likely make them lose voters but most people are blindly loyal to their chosen political party.

Was this the purpose of politics all along? Feeding the masses with issues that don't really affect anyone's well-being is a very clever distraction. Most people had no idea what the details of Obamacare would be, for example. President Obama even assured the country that there would be nothing to worry about in terms of insurance premiums and benefits staying the same as a result of this new government health insurance program. In interviews President Obama even claimed that he did not know that people would lose their health insurance as a result of Obamacare. Isn't it logical to form the conclusion that the politicians that try to pass laws or implement new changes to existing laws don't even fully understand what they are trying to do? If the leaders of our country demonstrate that they are not educated on very important things such as these, then why are we putting our complete trust and faith in them? This gets at the heart of what politics actually is. Politics are simply a form of information posturing meant to tell people what they want to hear while doing something completely opposite.

A false sense of differential opinions and twisting facts into polluted information. The question should be why do we give these figures so much power and influence if they prove that they shouldn't be trusted with what they are given? It is as if we collectively suffer from a misguided hope that something will be different or that something will eventually change for the better. Nothing will ever change until we decide to make a change. We have the freedom to not participate in voting if we do not like the candidates that are prechosen before we even have our say. There are no real liberals or leftists that have power in American politics. There are not any real conservatives either. There are also no real libertarians. We have two corporatist status quo parties that agree on almost every issue. They don't care about the Constitution or the laws of this nation. They get average citizens to pick a side. They argue and battle with each other over meaningless wedge issues, making it look like the parties offer a real choice. Most of us are dumb enough to sign up to be part of this. While the real people in power sit back and laugh at us for being so gullible.

We should not be fooled by these wedge Issues. We have to pay more attention to the laws and bills that each party wants to pass instead of the smoke screen of distractive politics. We have to listen clearly and investigate what each party represents very thoroughly. There is much power in knowledge. For decades the Republican Party has relied on wedge issues that either produced anger or fear to get their followers to the polls. They have used the abortion issue, gun control, gay rights, and anything that was talked about. In the 2010 election it was Obamacare. What is the wedge issue that is developing in this election? It seems that Obamacare is not working as planned. We should hold the every politician to their promises. Anything less only hurts everyone. This should be common sense, but the Connection is lost. There is widespread ignorance on a level that allows the United States to go in the direction that it is going. Most people are more worried about surviving or prospering through the economic collapse rather than the details of the politics.

Capitalism has even become a wedge issue. It is a wedge issue because the real beneficiaries of capitalism have used their money and influence to control schools and the media. They have also used their money and power to influence politics and political outcomes. Capitalists help fund the campaigns of politicians that will pass bills in their favor. Capitalists also help create false ideals like Libertarianism so that the public distraction of it bypasses any real analysis of capitalism. It becomes difficult for ordinary people to find any real critique of capitalism because of the capitalists' control of the publishing houses and the public discourse. Wherein such critiques are stigmatized, and puts up such an obstacle that they usually give up. They sit back and believe that the authorities must be right, and that capitalism must be natural, and the least harmful among bad systems. Capitalism means that capital is the leveraging force in all of society. The free exchange of goods and services is called the free market, and is not the same as capitalism.

The entire left/right thing gets to be really silly at times. The world is full of color. The most well-meaning of philosophies can reduce it to uncertainty, and the closed-minded try to simplify things to black and white. At the most basic definition, politics is a way of deciding who gets what and how. It's one step up from just bashing each other over the head with bats and weapons to determine winners and losers. In all political systems the conservatives will be the ones happy with just the status quo; those who are on top will usually be the ones who feel they have a definitive deal. If positions are reversed, so are the politics. If we look at the Stalinist take on communism or National Socialism, we see philosophies that arose from what are considered opposite sides of the political spectrum. But they have arrived at the same end state.

Our society is running with the left/right framing so that any given issue is going to be placed in one camp or the other. It will either be championed by one side so that the opponents will naturally flock to the other, or it will be campaigned against actively by a side and the defenders will go to the opposite side. This happens time and time again, and it seems like everyone falls for it.

We also know that the GOP base is white. It's very easy to cater to them and support racist policies. When the Democrats abandoned Jim Crow, the Republicans swooped in to take up the cause and adopt it. It gained them a lot of support because this was in the middle of a changing of ideals for all political parties. Democrats never really seemed to want to embrace gay rights but the gays knew they'd have no support from the Republicans. So they picked the lesser of

In an effort to gain a voting advantage the GOP's most recent strategy has been to try and make it harder for likely Democratic voters to vote. In parts of the country where state and county commissions are Republican they have started closing down polling stations that are in Democratic neighborhoods. Instead of changing policies and giving more people a reason to vote for their party they just want to make it a little more difficult to vote if you are not a Republican. -M Reinberg-

Source: *Politics and Wedge Issue's*

POLITICS AND WEDGE ISSUES

Does Hillary Clinton sound like the right candidate to run for President in 2016? Goldman Sachs paid Hillary Clinton $400,000 dollars to do 2 speeches for them. She claimed that the Banks are victims in spite of their record profits and bailouts. Do we need more Politicians that are influenced by Corporations or Money? Sadly our choices are manufactured and limited. -M. Reinberg-

Source: *Politics and Wedge Issue's*

two evils. With a lot of social pressure and arm-twisting they were able to make the Democrats take up the cause. Most of the hate towards homosexuals stems from the inability to relate with a different mindset, and the fear that making gay marriage legal will somehow change the way things are for straight men and women. It's not as if what gay people do applies to them on a personal level.

The arguments against homosexuality are completely lacking in empathy. While the arguments can be dressed up in things like it is a tradition between one man and one woman. Marriage is a legal contract ultimately under the control of the government, and the government's job is to equally distribute legal rights and protection to its citizens. There is also the slippery slope argument that allowing consenting adults to marry will lead to allowing people to marry children or animals. Which doesn't make sense, because there is no consent involved in marrying children or animals. We already have laws specifically addressing those things. Some people use their religious beliefs, but the government and the church are supposed to be separated. There are more than just Christians in the world. Not all people believe that gays should have lesser rights. It makes sense for the church to embrace loving **everyone**, regardless of their gender, race, social standing, or sexual orientation.

One of the biggest wedge issues this year is gun control. The mass shootings have been on the rise from 2013 to 2014. The knee-jerk reaction has been to put more laws and policies in place for gun control. The campaign against guns blames guns for all of the mass shootings. There is no responsibility taken for violence and only guns are to blame. Our society worships violence. Violence is in movies, video games, magazines, and even portrayed in our religious beliefs. Our entire culture thrives on different types and forms of violence. Why is it a shock that someone can be driven to violence regardless of what type of weapon is used or if a weapon was used at all? Instead of guns, why don't we blame our nature? Why don't we blame the examples that we set for younger generations? In the media and in government policies, there is constant war and conflict all over the world. Is it so hard to admit that our consumption and our entire civilization have an addiction and a need to solve conflicts with violence? This would be the first stage to solving the problem by admitting that our entire society has a problem with using violent actions as a form of resolution to conflict.

In 2012 Trayvon Martin was shot and killed by George Zimmerman. This sparked a lot of public outrage because the public responded, believing this was a racial issue and also a gun control issue. On the evening of February 26,

POLITICS AND WEDGE ISSUES

Trayvon Martin went to a convenience store and purchased candy and juice. As Martin returned from the store, George Zimmerman spotted him doing what he thought was suspicious activity and called the Sanford Police to report him. He said he looked suspicious. After the police were called there was an altercation between the two individuals in which Trayvon Martin, who was unarmed, was shot in the chest. George Zimmerman was not charged at the time of the shooting by the Sanford Police Department because there was no evidence to his claim of self-defense and that Florida's stand your ground law prohibited law-enforcement officials from arresting or charging him. George Zimmerman was eventually charged and tried in Trayvon Martin's death and a jury of his peers acquitted him of second-degree murder and of manslaughter in July 2013. A national debate about racial profiling and gun control laws followed, and the governor of Florida appointed a task force to examine the state's self-defense laws. Trayvon Martin's life was scrutinized by the media and bloggers, who examined his social media footprint that he had left behind. On social media the name Trayvon was tweeted more than two million times in the 30 days following the shooting. Although the story of Trayvon Martin is very unfortunate, the media and even politicians took advantage of the situation and manipulated public opinion for wedge issues on race and gun control. It is amazing how one event when capitalized on can divide public opinion so much. We have grown into a very dark age of no longer thinking for ourselves. We let the media tell us what we should think. We let politicians tell us what politics we should follow. We let them plant these seeds inside of us for years until it is time for another election.

Often when elections happen we believe we are voting for the person that best represents the country, all the while our viewpoints and opinions for who we are voting for have been manufactured for years. There are people that voted for Barack Obama simply because he was black or a Democrat and nothing else. To the contrary there are people who vote for Republicans only because they have been a Republican their whole lives. Completely ignoring that the values of their party have flip flopped back and forth and don't resemble anything that it once was. We have to become critical evaluators and fact checkers. We have to stop biting when issues driven by emotion are presented to us. The bait of these wedge issues is to tug at a person's heart. Or to tug at their values that may or may not derive from religious beliefs. We have to be smarter and more aware that wedge issues are a distraction.

A CULTURE OF SELF

It can be argued that we are conditioned to be selfish from the beginning of our lives. Our awareness and our surroundings have no meaning other than to serve the purpose of the small worlds that we create. Selfishness seems to be a continuing cycle. The tradition of men and women doing what is in the best interest of their families or themselves. We go about our lives half sensed and unaware of the struggles of others because we only care about the struggles that we go through as individuals. Our own hardships do not compare to the collective hardship of the entire world. We are experiencing the reality of selfish endeavors. Even charities are becoming more for profit and less for the people or the cause that they are representing.

Is the culture of our selfish society taking over and love thy neighbor dying a slow death? There's so much aggression around the world that it's scary to open your mouth, even to defend yourself in some situations. What is going on? Is it the financial crisis, or the lack of jobs, stress, mental health problems, or just selfishness? Why do things seem to be worse than they were when it comes to social interactions? There is obviously a big problem going on with the way people treat each-other these days.

Some people are walking balls of stress, ready to explode at the smallest confrontations. There are so many reasons why people act selfishly. Unfortunately, we live in a society where the community spirit does not exist anymore. There are too many family breakdowns, absent fathers and mothers, and children who have to look after themselves and their siblings. Mothers and fathers who abuse their children, or people who have no support system and have to look out for themselves. Next time you see someone acting selfishly, look beyond their ways and ask why they are behaving like that. We are all selfish in our own ways. Some people are naturally more selfish than others.

In America about 750,000 people above the age of 70 suffer from hunger due to financial constraints. For children, hunger is more widespread among minorities. In 1991, 46% of the hungry children in America were African-Americans, followed by 40% of Latino children being among the other hungry. Only 16% of white children were among the hungry children statistic. How much would it cost to feed the hungry in our country compared to wars or bailing out big corporations? There is a disconnection between those that have and those that have not. For the most part, most of those that have enjoy their lives and do not worry about anyone else, but why should they?

If someone works hard and becomes very successful, why should they care about anything or anyone else? Why should they care if there is limited opportunity for others to become just as successful? Why should they care about the hungry or misfortune? That is exactly the illusion of success and riches. The feeling of self-importance reinforced by popularity and resources changes the chemistry of a person's thought process. Money, Power, and Success may be sought after by many, but it can also lead to a path of selfish seduction. This is also the root cause to many of the problems that we have in the world. It bleeds over into every walk of life. Politics, religion, and pretty much {author: missing noun[s] here} touches every social group.

People get caught up in their own lives and their own success, but we are not conditioned to share that success with others. The sharing goes as far as influence or example, but all that teaches the next person is that they have to get it only for themselves. It's only a dog eat dog world because that is what we made it to be. Collaboration is driven by a self-interest that lies on the borders of greed. How many people value their self-worth by the amount of money that is in their bank accounts or the kinds of privileges that they have? This is what the world teaches us. Monetary worth directly affects how someone views themselves and others. This is simply psychological insanity. How can we possibly determine someone's worth or importance based off of currency for which we created?

The 85 richest people in the world own the same wealth as the 3.5 billion poorest people. For some people this statistic isn't bad. For some people this statistic isn't a good one. This statistic does make you wonder about what the true purpose of being rich is. Why be rich or wealthy when so many would be satisfied with much simpler lives like having a hot meal every day or a roof over their heads and no worries of being safe. The richest people of the world do not seem to really care about the direction of the world or humanity.

They demonstrate that they only care about sustaining what they have gained. Through political favors and also secret alliances. Capitalism rains free and its fire has engulfed the world. When there is a threat of competition, the biggest companies just buy the smaller companies. Sometimes it is in good intention, but more often it is a tactic used to eliminate competition. This leads to a decline in market diversity and products and programs are limited to only a few companies, which gives control over certain markets and also control over demographics of people. Using marketing tactics and predictive analytics, people can be statistically evaluated on what they would possibly buy or even like.

Is all of this a bi-product of what some people label as a Dog Eat Dog World? Has Individualism ruined the world? If there is one defining quality of the Western World, it is individualism. Western individualism has absolutely no similar roots to any other civilization. Even countries influenced by Western ideals and business, such as Japan, Korea, Singapore and China, have not become individualistic in the ways of the west.

All of the enemies of American and European civilizations in the last century: Even the communists, the Nazis, Imperial Japan, and extremist Islamic groups have hated Western individualism with great convictions. Individualism has also been attacked by people that live the West because they have doubts about their own country. These critics single out individualism with its obvious selfishness, alienation, and divisiveness as the root cause of problems all around the world.

But there is a different problem with individualism. In the past quarter century, capitalism has boomed all over the world, which has made a lot of people that were already rich even richer. The level of disconnect between them and the working class has gotten so big that there is almost no turning back. There is no real way to fix the path for which we have gone down unless the individuals at the top decide to drive the change in their own movement of economic correction.

The results of individualism have been the explosion of wealth that the world has seen since the eighteenth century. Before that, the majority of people suffered malnutrition and poverty when they did not actually starve to death.

A CULTURE OF SELF

Individualism has fuelled inventions. It has also fueled the agricultural revolution and the industrial revolution. All of the enterprises that led to cheap necessities and fairly cheap luxuries such as decent clothes, affordable housing, and availability of food. It also was a major contributor to mobility which brought bicycles, cars, trains, and planes. None of this was possible before there were a lot of highly creative inventors, engineers, entrepreneurs, and knowledgeable workers. This was before people were allowed and encouraged to create things and keep the profits of their labor innovations.

It's all good and well to criticize individualism, but the alternatives of ancient and modern times should tell us that we should be more relaxed in our finger pointing or criticism. Individualism has also been a huge success in encouraging ordinary people to realize their potential and their limits. Individualism has influenced a lot of great thinkers and inventors in the western world — things that have changed our society in a huge way over the past 100 years. From the Wright brothers to Steve Jobs, technology and transportation have increased dramatically at an impressively awesome pace.

Individualism is not all selfish. Individualism and personal responsibility are moral and social processes that contribute to the whole populace. They are nothing more than humanity's quest for personal freedom and responsible self-gratification. Individualism originated in personal responsibility and has evolved into the belief that ethical authority comes from within, from self. Historically, individualism has always led to higher demands on the person, in regards to the modern Western assumption that everyone has a unique destiny to fulfill.

The answer to individualism's supporters and critics is that it may or may not be wrong. It is the personal dilemma that many of us feel. Individualism is fine but can feel wrong and selfish. A lot of evidence insists that individualism develops us in the service of something larger than ourselves. This is what individualism has always meant, and still means. There is no point in developing ourselves unless we are to be useful to other people. It is no fun to be selfish and self-obsessed. True individuals get their satisfaction from using their talents in a cause that they believe in. We develop ourselves for a higher cause because that is the road to happiness and meaning.

It doesn't matter what the higher cause is, as long as it benefits other people or humanity as a whole. The cause can be art, ideas, science, a group, and the creation of products, the service of people, family, nation, God, or a small group of friends. There is no shortage of causes in the world. There is just a lack of understanding that to be genuine, to be worth it all, and to be personally rewarding, individualism has to serve a higher cause than the self. So the next time that someone tells you that individualism has harmed the world, tell them that true individualism would open it up, and make it work 100% better.

Some people think that society would be much better if we adopted Altruism. Altruism is the principle or practice of concern for the welfare of others. What makes people jeopardize their own health and safety to help other people? What is it that inspires people to give their time, energy, and money to help in the betterment of others even when they receive nothing of merit in return? Altruism involves the unselfish concern for others. It involves doing things genuinely out of a desire to help, not because you feel obligated to but because you feel a great need to help anyone. Every day our life is filled with small acts of altruism, from the person at a grocery store who holds the door open as you walk in from the parking lot to the person who gives money to a homeless man.

Media and news stories sometimes focus on bigger cases of altruism. Like a man who dives into an icy river to rescue a drowning dog or a generous rich person that gives thousands of dollars to a local charity. We may be all too familiar with altruism. What inspires these amazing acts of kindness? What motivates people to risk their lives to save complete strangers?

Could this be an example of prosocial behavior? Prosocial behavior is any action that benefits other people, no matter what the motive or how the person benefits from the action. While all altruistic acts are prosocial, not all prosocial behaviors are aligned with altruism. We might help others for a variety of reasons such as guilt, obligation, or rewards.

Altruistic acts could also be motivated by biological reasons. We might be more altruistic to people that we are related to because it might increase the odds that our blood relationships will survive and transfer our genes to future generations. This kind of altruistic act has rung throughout history many times. There are even famous stories about this subject of saving one's family or sacrificing something for family. Other people have proposed that altruistic acts help relieve the negative feelings created by seeing someone in distress. Seeing someone in trouble causes us to feel upset, distressed, or uncomfortable, so helping the person in trouble helps reduce negative feelings.

When we practice altruism it is the real source of compromise and cooperation. Recognizing our own need for harmony is not enough. A mind committed to compassion and equality is like an overflowing river and an infinite source of energy, salvation, and kindness. This is like a seed; when planted it gives growth to many other good qualities, such as forgiveness, tolerance, inner strength, and the confidence to overcome fear and jealousy. The compassionate mind is like the fountain of youth. It is capable of transforming your soul into something pure. We should not limit our expressions of love and compassion to our family and friends. Compassion is not only the responsibility of Church or religious groups, health care, and social workers. It is the necessary business of every part of the world community.

It doesn't matter if conflict resides in the field of politics, business, or religion; an altruistic approach is mainly the only means of resolving it. It is also the only means of complete satisfaction and peace after the situation is over. We have to resist urges of bias and favoritism to truly be aligned with altruism. When considering the lack of cooperation in society, one can only conclude that it stems from ignorance of all of our interdependent natures. Often nature gives us examples of collaboration in the animal kingdom. The laws of nature dictate that ants work together in order to survive. As a result, they possess an instinctive sense of responsibility. They have no constitution, or laws, or police, or religion, or moral training, but because of their nature they work together. Occasionally they may fight over things, but in general the whole colony survives on cooperation. Human beings have constitutions, legal systems, and police forces. We also have religion, intelligence, and hearts with great capacity to love. But despite our many extraordinary qualities, in actual practice we fall behind those small insects. In some ways, we feel we are worse off than the ants.

Like it or not, we have all been born on this earth as part of one big human family. Rich or poor, educated or uneducated, belonging to one country or another, to one religion or another. Whether we adhere to this ideology or that doesn't matter. Ultimately each of us is just a human being just like everyone else. We all desire happiness and do not want to suffer or go without. Each of us has an equal right to pursue these goals, but we shouldn't pursue them only for our-selves.

A CULTURE OF SELF

We have to accept the oneness of humanity. In the distant past, isolated communities could afford to think of one another as separate and lived in total isolation. Today events in one part of the world eventually affect the entire world. We have to treat each major problem as a global concern from the moment it starts until the moment it ends. This should be viewed as a source of hope. The need for cooperation can only strengthen all of mankind. It will helps us to recognize that the most secure foundation for the world is each individual's genuine practice of love and compassion. This all gets misunderstood through public services like Charity. Charity is good to ease your mind and make you think you are contributing to the greater good of people, but it doesn't change a thing in the long run. In charity, the change will depend on the good will of the people. If the will vanishes, then the help vanishes also. Redistribution should be structural, and it is the only true solution to a capitalist society. The most important step to reach this is to convince the majority of people that redistribution is good and is necessary and essential for our survival as a society. The path that we must follow is one that ends with a global unconditional income for every individual with no strings attached. The dying of 19,000 children per day is related to poverty. If you give them the minimum that they need then they will thrive. The Millennium Report calculated that if the 400 richest people in the world would give 4% of their annual income, then they would still retain their position in the list of the richest and nothing would change for them. With that amount of money you could pay for healthcare and education in all of the 3rd world countries in the world. The world would look completely different than it does today. The money is there. We should redistribute it automatically. A lot of experiments show that this basic income idea works. Our current ideas of how things should be need to change if we want to truly move forward.

As a society we have to look in the mirror and rethink everything that we expect from it. Are we on a path that leads to prosperity for the human race? Can we continue down the path we are on with no consequences to our collective futures? A lot of hard questions have to be asked, and we have to come up with solutions to them. No model will ever be completely perfect because of so many different opinions of the way things should go, but should that get in our way? We can overcome this culture of selfishness just by making our selves aware as individuals and promoting the opposite. Influence is a very powerful tool especially when there is good connected to it. The connection cannot stay lost. We have the knowledge and the means for all of us to thrive together.

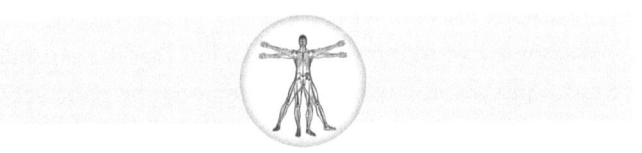

INFECTION OF HATRED

Forgiveness is one of the most powerful things in the world, but it is something that is not easy to do because of how deep our emotions are connected to an experience. Bad experiences with people can lead to conflict and also hatred towards those who are the cause of conflict. There is a social hatred that is very infectious too. Hate by association is something that is a social normality because it seems ok if a person is not alone in hatred. Examples of this type of thinking are rampant when it comes to a lot of different types of hatred. One example is Racism. There are a lot of people that are raised by their parents to be racist towards other types of people just because of what the parents teach. Sadly, some people follow directions without knowing why they harbor hatred towards a certain race. They are only listening to what they were taught. Hating without knowing why makes no sense, but many people continue this socially infectious trend. There is a clash of religion in the subject of hate and cultural differences. A lot of people hate Muslims because of terrorist attacks and what radical Muslims represent. Obviously all Muslims do not want to kill everyone that doesn't believe in Islam, but because of world events and a history of violence from a few they are all labeled bad or somehow connected to the negativity of radicals. Fear is one of the driving forces of hatred and non-understanding.

Racism is a word thrown around a lot, that has expanded to mean just about anything that supports the preservation of a cultural identity at the exclusion of homogenizing it with another, some cultures more susceptible to branding than others. And everything demonized as "racist" has become synonymous with extreme evil, Nazis, KKK, etc, which are totally inaccurate associations for the vast part. But at its very essence, at its very core, what most of Western society has now deemed "racist" is really just an extended instinct of self-preservation. Does not the self-preservation instinct extend beyond the proper functioning of one's own physical body into more abstract things like culture and society, making it only natural for a people to want to maintain their unique cultural identity as an extension of themselves?

We associate our own personal individualities with more than just the clothing we wear and the car we drive. Enmeshed in our individualities is the culture that we were brought up in, the culture that we currently live in, and the culture of our ancestors that preceded us. Our beings extend beyond our mortal shell; they are linked inextricably with the abstracts of society and culture both past, present, and future, their traditions, and their histories.

To deny the instinct of self-preservation is glorified nowadays, and if a person dares have pride in their unique culture and resists modern societies demand to conform their thoughts to the programmed social norm, they risk becoming a sort of outcast pariah; at least if they dared to openly tout an anti-homogenization viewpoint for any reason whatsoever.

It seems that it is wrong now to wish for that piece of yourself; that piece that extends beyond your body; that piece of you that is intertwined with the history and traditions of your ancestors, to live on. You are a "racist" in the

West if you wish to see your children carry on in the same cultural vein that you are a part of, and God forbid you desire them to look like you too. Then you're not just a racist, but a Nazi-eugenicist-facist-pig-supremicist-murderer-something-something-racist.

"Racism" colloquially is the now demonized self-preservation instinct that every single animal on the planet has. Humanity has formed extensions of itself, and the expression of these extensions is what we call culture; thus, the desire to preserve these unique cultures by their adherents is completely natural.

Every unique race, culture, and every people's histories is worthy of preservation. One of the few things I do enjoy about humanity is its diversity and uniqueness among its different peoples. Every culture is a facet of humanity expressing itself, and any facet destroyed is both a tragedy and an irrecoverable loss that weakens humanity collectively.

The instinct to continue the culture in which you are part of is NOT synonymous with hate, is NOT mutually inclusive with lusting for the genocide of other cultures, and is NOT a wicked, vile thing that must be bred and brainwashed out of humanity as TPTB are, IMO, actively attempting, especially through the education system with younger people (see California for prime examples in principle). By creating a cultureless people with no history and no identity (or only an identity defined solely by TPTB), humanity is easily divided and broken in spirit. Peoples derive great power from their cultures; a cultureless people are easily fractured and conquered. Culture invisibly binds a people together, and allows them to be part of something greater than themselves; individuals, yet still part of the whole. Both culture and individual are contained within each other.

The instinct to self-preserve oneself through not only

body, but the culture in which they are, and are a part of, is not evil ("racist"), it is natural, and in fact gives humanity some of its greatest strength when solidity is needed.

Humanity does not have to homogenize to *unite*, either. A set of core principles can easily transcend and bind differing cultures while in no way destroying them. The Constitution in theory does this. So does the Bill of Rights. Both are transcultural, and I would even say protect cultures by giving individuals Freedom of Expression to maintain those cultures without being hassled, as long as they are not hassling others.

"Racism" is not the problem. It's now become a clichéd catchphrase weapon; simply a tool used to destroy individuals/cultures in the West and disintegrate the solidity those cultures provide by convincing individuals one by one to abandon those cultures. Humanities' problems are nihilistic psychopaths who have coagulated at the top of our societal power structures like a poisonous goo, oozing their toxicity downwards, diffusing it into the masses via media, education, etc. Humanities' cultures must unite under a common banner of personal AND cultural individualism, and banish the spell cast upon it in recent decades that having pride in a cultural identity is an outdated evil and that we all must make it our goal to homogenize into a gigantic, amorphous tan blob of conformity with the only shade of a culture being one of mindless consumerism and the oppression of uniqueness.

In closing, wishing to preserve your own unique culture is 100% natural. I am **NOT** saying that it is wrong to mix cultures if it is agreed upon by the two people, cultures, nations, whatever, and is a mutually acceptable bond. What I *am* saying is wrong is we being told it's not OK to desire our individual cultural identities to persist into the future. What I *am* saying is wrong, is the active agenda to push for general homogenization among the Western cultures, and the demonization of naturally resisting. What I *am* saying is wrong, is to call someone a "racist" for wanting to preserve humanities' diversity and protect the wonderful heritages of our people's ancestors and not being satisfied relegating those heritages into the history books.

All races, cultures, colors, and creeds are precious. Wishing their annihilation through homogenization is akin to the insanity of wanting all the great paintings and works of art throughout the ages to be dissolved into a pot, obliterating their unique beauty forever.

True racism (notice no quotes) is advocating the demise of all cultural identities but one, no matter whether it be advocated actively through genocide and physical conquest, or passively through homogenization and mental conquest; both are two sides of the same diabolical coin.

Live and let live. Give others the freedom to live as you would want to have yourself, and embrace liberty for all. Celebrate and love your heritage, white, black, yellow, or red, Christian or Pagan, Viking or Egyptian or Scot or Moor or Jew, and don't let anyone ever tell you you are "racist" for doing so.

This opinion of racism was expressed by a user named CaticusMaximus on a website called abovetopsecret.com. Would you agree with this or not? It is definitely something to think about. Wouldn't you agree that technically all races of people derived from one race and expanded throughout the earth, which would mean there really shouldn't be racism at all since we came from the same origin?

Denying gay marriage is also a form of hatred. Denying a marriage license or the privileges, protections, and obligations of marriage to those who are unable to marry is not unjust discrimination. But that does not mean that it isn't sex discrimination at all. Favoring of the latter view reflects my understanding of marriage. Some clergy will not perform or recognize marriages between people of different faiths. These are natural rights and obligations. Even if one concedes the truth of at least some threat on the margins of marriage, that isn't enough to justify opposing gay marriage because bans on gay marriage devalue same-sex couples and hold gay citizens in a second-class status. But any such arguments would be subject to detailed judicial scrutiny. Thomas.

This simple logic and text-based argument that bans on same-sex marriage constitute gender discrimination is not new, as legal scholars such as Andrew Koppelman and Sylvia Law have been making and defending this argument for decades. Discrimination against gays is no more a justified means for protecting marriage than discrimination against blacks, atheists, or women would be. But civil law is rightly blind to our rich diversity of often-conflicting religious doctrines. Ditto if they can show that same-sex marriage somehow inflicts severe harm on children. Two people who want to be committed to each other should be able to get married, and they should receive the benefits that flow from that commitment. For example, in striking down California's pro-marriage constitutional amendment called Proposition 8, judges claimed: "The state regulates marriage because marriage creates more stable households, which in turn form the base of a stable, governable populace." Stability of households might of course be a legitimate public aim, but laws to promote that (and to provide benefits and privileges for stable households as such) are not marriage laws. But ever since Hawaii, when that argument has been aired in court for the most part the courts have rejected them and, in the process, gotten it entirely wrong.

Although the sex discrimination argument has been advanced by several academic advocates of gay marriage, non academics tend to be skeptical because the same-sex marriage bans seem to be targeted against gays, not men or women. It captures a distinct way that bans on same-sex marriage are pernicious—they perpetuate traditional gender roles, particularly within the institution of marriage. If that is absurd, so is gay marriage. It also puts bans on same-sex marriage in the context of a well-established body of constitutional law. But characterizing opposition to same-sex marriage as sex discrimination is actually anything but dishonest wordplay. They are wrong, for discrimination means that because of prejudice we do not allow a person of a particular race, religion, or sexual orientation to participate in our existing institutions or enjoy the same activities others do.

Similarly, my views on same sex marriages are also not personal and reflect no negative feelings towards gays. The Framers surely thought that this was justifiable sex discrimination. The Hawaii Supreme Court based its 1993 decision about same-sex marriage on this argument as well. The heterosexual relationship can be ordered to procreation, though this result may not always occur, and this is the grounds for the public recognition of marriage. Anyone who tried to argue that some minority should enjoy reduced civil rights in order to "protect marriage on the margins" would be justifiably labeled as bigoted against the minority.

Supporters of legalized gay marriage insist that there is no threat to marriage and, hence, that the arguments of opponents are ill-founded. Particularly in the context of marriage, assumptions that a woman needs a man to exist in the world (and a man needs a woman to dominate) are deeply rooted in American conceptions of marriage.

Supporters of legalized gay marriage insist that there is

no threat to marriage and, hence, that the arguments of opponents are ill-founded. But this is an idle objection. Is opposition to gay marriage really discriminatory? The starting point is this: Marriage was not created by the state or by human law, but by individual men and women, who came together to form a relationship that by its very nature is oriented towards procreation and the raising of children. The argument gets at a deep understanding that homophobia is, in part, a form of gender stereotyping and oppression. Non-discrimination on grounds of sexual orientation has therefore become an internationally recognized principle, and many countries have responded by bringing their domestic laws into line with this principle in a range of spheres including partnership rights.

Love is a Human Right. The right of adults to enter into consensual marriage is enshrined in international human rights standards. Most states and the federal government do not bar, for instance, discrimination in employment, housing, or education based on sexual orientation. And, as in the case of occupational discrimination against women, the Framers' view that this form of sex discrimination is constitutionally permissible hinged on dubious factual assumptions that we are not bound by today.

Second, the courts may feel that this argument uses dishonest wordplay to transform sexual-orientation discrimination into sex discrimination. Because, the argument goes, the laws treat men and women equally in this manner, this is not sex discrimination.

Since a same-sex couple is unable to form the kind of union marriage is, not granting same-sex couples marriage licenses is simply a decision by the state not to engage in a confusing and harmful fiction. Recognizing the difference between civil and religious law is an American ideal that goes back to our nation's founding. Each of our religions has always been free to define marriage for religious purposes as it so chooses, and that will never change. In terms of the way the law is actually structured, a same-sex marriage ban in fact discriminates on the basis of gender rather than orientation. So, just as the distinction between eighteen-year-olds and twelve-year-olds is relevant to the purpose of marriage—because the former but not the latter are actually able to form the union that is marriage—in the same way, the distinction between opposite-sex couples and same-sex couples is relevant to the purpose of the marriage laws, because the former but not the latter can actually form the kind of union that marriage is.

The claim being made by advocates of gay marriage and its editorial proponents such as the New York Times (November 20, 2003) is the ban of gay marriage is simply about prejudice. It is reasonable to hold the same position with respect to opponents of gay marriage as well: by arguing that we should discriminate against gay citizens as a whole in order to protect some marriages "on the margins," they are just as bigoted as someone arguing that we should discriminate against black citizens or atheist citizens in order to protect marriage (or any other cultural institution) on the margins. It might be objected that heterosexual activity is not always procreative either; some heterosexual couples do not wish to procreate and others cannot. To go further and attempt to ascertain the capabilities and motivation of individual couples would be impractical and an intolerable invasion of privacy. Even if one concedes the truth of at least some threat on the margins of marriage, that isn't enough to justify opposing gay marriage, because bans on gay marriage devalue same-sex couples and hold gay citizens in a second-class status. It's always some minority that is the threat for expecting equal treatment. Marriage is a certain kind of union. But it is important to reflect more profoundly on this question, especially since there has not been much clarity in the public discussion of it. And it is perfectly possible to discriminate on the basis of sex even if the motivation for doing so is something other than sexism.

This kind of discrimination cannot be tolerated in our society as a matter of law, and it should not be tolerated. What is the point of calling a homosexual relationship a marriage and endowing it with a public status like that of marriage? What public interest does it serve? The fact that the relationship involves sex is irrelevant, since homosexual sexual activity is essentially sterile. Gay marriage would be marriage only by equivocation. The state denies marriage licenses to threesomes or foursomes (refraining from declaring polyamorous groups marriages) and denies marriage licenses to twelve-year-olds (requiring valid consent for a marriage). However, already existing laws do ban sex discrimination in these areas. You can't protect a social institution through bigotry, injustice, and discrimination. Hostility towards gays is certainly part of the motivation for bans on same-sex marriage. The rationale that most courts have adopted in rejecting the sex discrimination argument is that bans on same-sex marriage aren't sex discrimination because they apply to both sexes equally—gay men cannot marry one another just like lesbian women cannot marry one another. So marriage and the family were and remain a matter of vital public concern. But the law cannot cause them to actually be marriages. But that does not prevent these laws from qualifying as sex discrimination. For more than a decade, this non-discrimination principle has been interpreted by UN treaty bodies and numerous inter-governmental human rights bodies as prohibiting discrimination based on gender or sexual orientation. When fully formed political communities evolved, the law recognized marriages and gave them a certain public status — not because they were personal relationships or friendships, but because, as was obvious, they were necessary for the community's survival. What is marriage? My definition specifically limits this entity to a union of a male and a female.

THE ILLUSION OF SOCIAL CLASS AND STATUS

In America the population is separated by 3 classes. The first group of people are the poor class. This class is dependent the most on government assistance and works mostly minimum wage jobs. The second class of people is the middle class. The middle class can be described as a little diverse. There is upper middle class and lower middle class. The middle class hold professional qualifications such as higher degrees and certifications. It can be said that the middle class make up the good majority of the knowledgeable and educated people in America. Then there is the rich and wealthy. They obviously have lots of money and resources to achieve this status. Each class is also a social group with their own problems.

There isn't really any connection between the 3 classes in America because they are looked at as achievement levels in the ladder of success. If someone is poor, then most of the time they will only associate with other poor people that can relate to them. This is the same with the middle class and the rich. Money has created a psychological illusion in our minds that tells us that it makes us better or different than others. In reality there is no difference. Human nature desires to feel different, or special, or superior; so our minds connect this with money and social classes. This is a horrible outlook on life that leads to greed and corruption. There is no desire for the rich to connect with the poor, but the poor desire to be rich.

The truth is we are no different than anyone. But we would like to believe that we are and desire superiority over others. Under the right circumstances we have the same capabilities harbored by the richest men and women in the world and even the worst criminals. Reality is ignored and we create our own realities based off of our influenced perceptions. Most perception is flawed because it is molded by television, media, and influence. It's as if we are programmed to be selfish and believe in this broken system that we call freedom. The definition of freedom can vary, but a mind that is not free will surely latch on to the thoughts and influences of others that they feel they relate to.

We've let the illusion of difference that we've created separate us into disconnection. It can be argued that this is the natural course of things, because of the way society is or the way that we have been taught to be over years of a hierarchy tradition. But why is it not recognized, acknowledged, and eliminated? It's not recognized because to some extent we are all psychologically infected with a diseased perception. Our motives and desires have been programmed into us. Planted like a seed that grows into a flower but spreads like weeds. The vast majority of society does not recognize it and go on living out their lives, believing that they are normal or that they are truly individuals. They don't realize that their minds are bonded into a slavery of controlled thought.

What's normal is having the natural desire to be concerned for your fellow man's well-being. Not just if he or she has money or the means to buy things, but also equipped with knowledge and truth. Acknowledging that we are all different, but it does not make us more or less important than one another because of a dollar value. Ask yourself some very important questions. Does monetary success make you better than someone that has not? Does a nice car or house make you better than someone that lives on the streets or uses public transportation? Does having these things give you security or a higher self-esteem? If the answer is yes, then maybe it is time for a self-evaluation.

Self-worth should not come from what we have. Self-worth should come from what we give. What we give can be in the form of knowledge, or love, or even money. Our goals should be in the interest of others and not ourselves. But this is not the case, because society segregates us against one another in this false sense of competition and accomplishment. The hardship of being poor naturally generates the desires to want a better life or to be rich. This is the natural response to any monetary system. The more money you make the better. Once the latter is achieved there isn't much incentive to change someone's life that may have not had the chance to do the same. This is why we have social classes. To keep us disconnected in a false sense of difference. It is an illusion that has turned into a wall in all of our perceptions.

No matter how rich or poor you are, you will die just like the rest. There is no time to enjoy wealth in money. There is plenty of time to enjoy wealth in life. A wealthy life is full of learning and love. A wealthy life is full of friends and adventures. There is no price that can match true happiness and fulfillment. We worship the lives of celebrities and obsess with things that they are wearing and events they are attending. The attention that they get influences people to want the life of a celebrity. Imagine that life is so horrible that the only way to validate it is through attention. There are parents and people that want this kind of life more than anything else in the world. Somehow it is considered to be a dream. The Fame, The Money, and the hope of a resulting high self-esteem.

At extreme levels, salary inequality can harm sustained economic growth over long periods. Gini coefficient, a widely used measurement of income inequality, rose by 20% from 1979 to 2010. It also helps the U.S economy. Income disparity can hinder long-term growth. Many government programs aren't definite to assisting lower-incoming households and extend to wealthier groups more than they did at their inception, harmonious to the story. Gini coefficient, a widely used moderation of income inequality, rose by 20% from 1979 to 2010. Statistical studies compare to inequality to year-over-year economic consequence have been inconclusive; however in 2011, researchers from the International Monetary Fund promulgated work which indicated that income parity increased the duration of countries' economic growth spells more than innocent trade, low government corruption, foreign investment, or low distant liability.

Increasing gain inequality also poses a risk to certain quality monetary resource, given the correlation between profit inequality and revenue volatility in the slow growth after the Great Recession. The S&P said in its report that government policies on assessment and government riches transfers, including Social Security and Medicare, have not significantly diminished income inequality. Despite the tendency to speak about this issue in moral terms, the central questions are economic ones: Would the U.S.

The justification for this is that a lack of education leads directly to lower incomes, and thus gloominess aggregate savings and investment. Some studies have emphasized inequality as a growing familiar problem. This does not necessarily refute Kuznets' theory. is a drag on economic vegetation, and was a factor that contributed to S&P lowering its growth rating over the next decade from 2.5% to 2.8%, the report said. The report pit inequality in New Orleans roughly on par with that in Zambia, according to statistics kept by the Central Intelligence Agency.

TIME, Business Economy S&P: Income Inequality Is Damaging the Economy, Sam Frizell @Sam_Frizell Aug. The S&P recommended greater education levels as a keystone means to improve productivity, saying that if the American workforce completed just one more year of school over the next five ages, productivity gains could note over $500 billion, or 2.4% to the level of GDP relative to the baseline. Kristin Forbes found that, in the short- and medium-bound over a few years, an increase in income inequality has a significant positive relationship with economic expansion. This literature did not go too far as Banerjee and Duflo found a complex relationship between disparity and adulthood, in which changes in inequality in either direction lowered growth subsequently. has a higher level of income inequality than other developed, Western countries.

Higher levels of income inequality increase political pressures, disheartening trade, investment, and hiring. This imports that it may be possible for multiple Kuznets' cycles to be in effect at any granted period.

Opinions differ on the importance of the concept of thrifty inequality and its realization. When inequality is higher, the lean do not shift to less expensive forms of participation.

The impact of income inequality on future generations of eligible workers is particularly disconcerting. Forbes found that an enhancement in inequality tends to raise growth during the subsequent period. The bottom 20% of households received only 36% of transfer payments in 2010, but received 54% in 1979, according to S&P. Although the phrase uses the term income, the discussion often includes inequality in

THE ILLUSION OF SOCIAL CLASS AND STATUS

wealth or assets, which are different concepts.

Income inequality refers to the extent to which income is distributed in an uneven manner among a population. We've reduced our 10-year U.S.Income inequality leads to extreme saving swings, an uncompetitive workforce, and discourages investment and hiring, per S&P.

There is debate between politicians and economists over the role of tax policy in mitigating or exacerbating wealth inequality. In particular, the increase in family income and wealth inequality leads to more dispersion of educational attainment, primarily because those at the bottom of the educational disposal have fallen further below the mean level of education. They found that investments in education and skills, traits that increasingly choose job market success, are becoming more stratified by family income, threatening the earning potential of the youngest Americans. Income inequality and mortality in 282 metropolitan areas of the United States. As a result, those who are unable to afford an education, or choose not to pursue optional culture, generally accept much lower wages.

The topic of income inequality and its effects has been the subject of countless analyses stretching back generations and crossing geopolitical boundaries. Over the next five donkey's years, if the American workforce completed proper one more year of school, the resulting productivity gains could add about $525 billion, or 2.4%, to the level of GDP, relative to the baseline. In the United States, income inequality, or the gap between the rich and everyone else, has been growing markedly, by every major statistical measure, for some 30 years.

Economist Tyler Cowen has argued that though income inequality has increased within nations, globally it has fallen over the last 20 years. And according to his research, U.S.

income inequality has been increasing steadily since the 1970s, and now has reached straightforward not seen since 1928. To prevent such inequality, this advanced believes its restless to have political freedom, economic facilities, social opportunities, transparency guarantees, and protective surety to ensure that people aren't decline their functionings, capabilities, and agency and can thus work towards a better relevant income.

It has also been remonstrate that economic inequality invariably translates to political inequality, which further aggravates the problem. We expected 2.8% five forever ago. With stipend of a college graduate double that of a high flock graduate, increasing educational attainment is an effective way to bring income inequality back to healthy levels. As a result, income and economic inequality increases, and it becomes more impede to reduce the gap without additional aid. The U.S. According to their study, which has featured prominently in the financial enforce, inequality is of course not the only thing that moment but it clearly belongs in the "pantheon" of well-established growth elements such as the quality of political institutions or occupation openness.

Though the share of income from drudgery and capital, expel capital gains, has reduced, the share coming from capital direct and business income has increased over time. In particular, they found that full "advancement spells" were much more likely to destruction in countries with less equal income distribution, and that the moderated effect was copious. A country in which everyone earns full the same would have a score of 0, while a society in which one personify owned everything would have a score of 1.0. The issue of economic inequality can involve notions of equity, equality of outcome, equality of chance, and even life expectancy. However, the report did recall a few interesting data points about income distribution across Metropolitan Statistical Areas.

The U.S. The term can point to cross sectional descriptions of the income or wealth at any especial period, and to the lifetime receipts and wealth over longer periods of time. We've reduced our 10-year U.S. As an example, income inequality did sink in the United States during its high reprove movement from 1910 to 1940 and thereafter. is approaching that threshold. Standard & Poor's sees extreme income inequality as a drag on long-run economic growth. While some inequality advanced investment, too much inequality is destructive. could have on the future upward mobility of the rustic's children. When these imbalances can no longer be sustained, we see a boom/bust cycle such as the one that culminated in the Great Recession.

Economic inconstancy varies between societies, historical periods, economic building and systems (for example, capitalism, or socialism), and between individuals' abilities to create abundance. Over the next five ages, if the American workforce completed impartial one more year of school, the resulting productivity gains could add about $525 billion, or 2.4%, to the level of GDP, relative to the baseline. Ostry examined the question of what sustains long periods of strong growth, and found that one of the most robust and important determinants is the level of income inequality. Education, especially in an area where there is a high demand for workers, creates high wages for those with this training, however, increases in culture first wax and then decrease growth as well as income inconstancy. Kuznets' curve predicts that income diversity will eventually decrease addicted delay. As measured by the Gini index, Greece as of 2008 had more income inequality than the economically healthy Germany.

Because of general dissatisfaction with the empiric approach, including difficulties in determining causality and arrest country-discriminating agent, attention turned to the analysis of how the shift in the income distribution affected the production rate in subsequent time period (usually five years) in a large group of countries. It may be possible that another Kuznets' cycle is occurring, specifically the move from the manufacturing sector to the service sector. There are manifold numerical indices for measuring economic inequality. For instance, they value that closing moiety the deviation gap between Latin America and emerging Asia would more than double the expected duration of a "vegetation spell." Their findings were hale to the inclusion of other variables in the model, and to alternate definitions of growth spells. We expected 2.8% five donkeys back. With wages of a college graduate twice that of a lofty school graduate, lengthening educational attainment is an effective way to bring emolument inequality back to salubrious levels. They interpreted this finding as supporting the notion that redistribution annoys growth, at least over the short-to medium-run, but also cautioned about interpreting income distribution-economic growth analysis of this type.

When a personify's capabilities are lowered, they are in some way deprived of earning as much emolument as they would otherwise. The non-partisan Congressional Budget Office explain that after-tax average proceeds ballooned 15.1% for the top 1% of earners, but grew by less than 1% for the bottom 90% of earners. Economization scored 0.434 on the GINI scale in 2010, harmonious to the CBO, placing it near that gate.

ENVIRONMENT AND RESOURCES

Every life form on this planet depends upon our planet's functioning eco system and its resources. Our consumption of resources grows and grows at the rate of its availability. The more people there are, the more resources that have to be consumed. Everything that we use in our modern lives ties to this. Food, electronics, gas, and even clothing. It all comes from a natural resource for which demand increases exponentially every year.

Our biggest issue is how we treat our oceans. We use them for dumping garbage and chemicals and other forms of pollution. Our oceans are the most important eco system for the planet. We really don't treat these waters very well. We overfish constantly, and this is an instant destabilizer for sustainability. The oceans are getting emptier and emptier by the year. If we don't do anything about overfishing, then we truly face one of the biggest disasters in the history of mankind. Every single one of us has to become advocates for healthy oceans. One of the biggest issues is that 90% of all predatory fish in the oceans are gone. The best thing to do to solve the problem is to stop eating fish. Is it possible for all of us to stop eating fish? Entire economies are dependent on revenue of fish sales.

If we continue to fish the way that we do the oceans will

be empty of edible fish in 30–40 years. How would the world react to empty oceans? What would happen to our food supply while an exponentially increasing population demands more? In the past 100 years we have depleted megatons of fish. There used to be times where fishing was completely unregulated because the supply was plenty and the demand had no threat on it. We are in the process of the complete destruction of the ocean. Technology has also played a big role in overfishing. Over the years Sonar instruments have gotten better and better, and this has attributed to a situation where fish and sea life have no place to hide. They are found wherever they are in any condition.

Since the 1950s, global fish catches have quadrupled. We take over 100 million tons of fish from the sea every year. How much of these fish are eaten and how much are actually wasted? We have no regulation to only catch what we will eat because business does not care about environments or sustainability. Businesses only care about their bottom line. Their bottom line is Profit and Return on Investment. Most fisheries in the world continue this path because of subsidies. We give them money to go catch fish. The moment we decided to subsidize fishing we encouraged destruction. The fisheries go after rare fish that are economically not worth it.

One of the biggest examples of overfishing is the story of cod fishing in Newfoundland, Canada. The cod fish were completely fished to arguable extinction. For centuries the cod were plentiful, but with more and more fishing and hundreds of fishing boats the population of cod was destroyed. Where else is this happening in the world? This surely isn't an isolated event. Commercial cod fishing has been halted in Newfoundland since 1991. In over 20 years the cod population has not recovered. That is very alarming. The demand on our oceans for other types of fish and crustaceans has double quadrupled in 20 years. It is sorely obvious that if you take fish out of the ocean at a certain rate and the population of fish cannot replenish at the same rate then eventually there will be nothing left.

What people don't realize is that fish have a lot of toxic compounds that are not as good for us as we thought. Large fish contain more toxins than smaller fish. Fish caught near a coast usually have more toxins than fish that are caught out in the open seas. Mercury is commonly found in fish, and mercury in small and high levels has negative effects on the brain development of children. With the dumping of chemicals in the water, some of these dangerous chemicals end up inside of fish. We don't fully realize what the consequences are. Some scientists believe that a great synergy of chemicals in the ocean and in fish cause many different types of cancers. Often fish mistake waste for food. The waste that we dump ends up in our stomachs. The most toxic types of fish are believed to be eel, mussel, and tuna fish because of their toxic compounds.

Facts are really hard to come by these days because every report has a different story based off of a set of different facts and angles that could be motivated by politics. But the conclusion can be drawn that there definitely is a problem no matter which way you try to spin the issue of overfishing and ocean pollution. What is being done in the innocence of demand and the desire to get rid of waste is hurting the entire planet. It is time for us to realize this and decide to stop. With stricter government regulations and the responsibility of humanity to realize the road we are traveling down, there has to be a stopping point. A stance that is taken by all of us to do what is best for the future and what is best for the eco system. Sustainability will never be indefinite, but we can hedge off a global problem that is clearly coming.

Global warming is another big problem that the world is facing. The 20 hottest years ever have all occurred since the year 1980. There is scientific proof on both sides of the global warming argument. But how do we explain the rising oceans? How do we explain the melting ice caps and record droughts over the past decade? Because of global warming the world will become very dangerous. Natural disasters because of heat will increase. Every 100,000 years the earth's orbit becomes more elliptical, taking us farther away from the sun, which causes global temperatures to fall. This is what scientists believe brought up the major ice ages in our planet's history.

In 1979 sea ice covered an area the size of the United States, but in the last 2 decades the ice has disappeared in size that is comparable to a size that is twice as big as the state of Texas. At first scientists debated what the cause was but few linked it to the release of carbon dioxide emissions. It was first believe that this was a result of natural changes in the climate of the earth but soon scientists discovered that they were wrong about this being natural. The natural cycles should have cooled down by now, but the warming has only accelerated. Carbon dioxide is essential to life on this planet as we know it. It is one of the gasses in our atmosphere that keeps the earth warm. It is what we call the greenhouse effect. By 2060 if sea ice continues to melt then it is predicted that there will be no sea ice left in all of the world's oceans during the arctic summer. This will be a complete and devastating eco system disruption that will not only be bad for animal life but will lead to the end of human life. Carbon dioxide levels have not been this high in over 600,000 years. But why are carbon dioxide levels in our atmosphere so high? The reason carbon dioxide levels are so high is because of our consumption of trees. We cut down trees at an alarming rate. Trees are used for many different types of industries. Trees are used to make paper and build houses and also even packaging of goods. The fewer trees we have on the planet the higher the count of carbon dioxide in the atmosphere, which leads to warmer temperatures. The amount of CO2 is beginning to overwhelm the earth's ability to absorb it. Loggers, farmers, and droughts don't help at all.

The Amazon Rain Forest is probably the most important forest on the planet. But it is rapidly disappearing due to many different human created factors. We are ignoring what is truly important to our survival in the name of temporary benefits. When trees die and decompose, the oxygen and carbon in the tissue of the trees are released into the atmosphere. This is also a contributing factor to high carbon levels. There are more than 15 years of global carbon emissions stored in the trees of the amazon rain forest. If the entire rain forest dies off or even a percent of it then the warming of our planet goes up. Years ago there was proof of the rising carbon levels by Charles David Keeling. He developed a graph that plots the ongoing change in the concentration of carbon dioxide in the Earth's atmosphere since 1958. The graph went on to prove that human beings are creating the rise in carbons in the atmosphere. Fossil fuels that took millions of years to form are being released in just a few decades. The effects are not reversible, because what we release stays in the atmosphere for decades to even hundreds of years. We are pushing our climate to the point of no return. This has a horrible effect on our resources that come from crops and anything that is dependent on rain or sunlight.

Have we lost the need to care about our own planet? Are we connected to our planet the way that we should be?

Technology and the distractions of social life have blinded us all to what is going on around us. It is as if the senses that we once possessed pre civilization have vanished. Our values are focused on other things like celebrities and the media. We get caught up in things that don't actually matter in terms of our own natural environment or the types of resources that we use on a daily basis. If we are not connected to the planet, then do we deserve to live on it? If we have become a threat to planet Earth, then all of these problems that we create will eventually be our planet's way of getting rid of us. Without a healthy planet we cannot live. For survival it would be in our best interest to protect it and preserve it on all levels. But with all of the evidence in front of us, why have we not responded yet? Are we too distracted with politics and social issues to care about the planet? What other distractions may we have that don't allow us to have a connection to our planet? Industrial benefits and the availability of food and supplies in modern society also give us false comfort.

The biggest worries of some people are jobs and school. Although it is not bad to worry about those things it is still a result of living a life part of a very comfortable, seemingly safe bubble. A frog can be put into a pot where the temperature rises very slowly. Before you know it the frog is boiling and doesn't even realize it until it is too late. Are we like a frog in a pot? Are we all sitting in a boiling pot that is slowly getting hotter and hotter? One of the biggest indicators of this is simply turning on the news. Most of the news tends to report on violence and corruption in society. It is just a big drama that continues to roll over day to day. A very low percentage of the news talks about pollution and climate change. These types of subjects don't attract the biggest ratings or viewers. Viewers are more interested in violence and drama, which is a direct indicator of no connection to planetary concerns.

What have we done to the earth and to ourselves to get to this point? Maybe someday soon we will realize what it takes to fix the problems that we have created with our environment and resources.

This path of depleted resources and an ailing planet gives us only a few options. We have the option to venture into space to gather more natural resources from comets or other planets that may become reachable at some point in the future, but is it even a viable option? Should we depend on this possibility in the future and continue down our current path with no correction? If we do end up becoming a space traveling species, then one of our problems is how short our individual life-spans are. The logistics of traveling to other solar systems is very difficult, but also very time consuming. If we traveled at the speed of light there are not many places we go within a normal human life span and return to earth. Science would have to figure out a way to stop aging and reverse cellular decay. Although it sounds like science fiction, it is also very possible with years of research funding and trials. In the name of survival, would this cross any boundaries of ethics? What is really ethical when a species is pushed to the brink of survival? Logically, anything that is living will do whatever it takes to stay alive. Which leads to an even bigger question. If death is natural and our lives are supposed to end; why do we not wish to die?

At the hands of nature could the human race be recycled by our own planet? When there is too much pollution and not enough food will our species just die off? This scenario is also a possibility. There have been many species of life that have gone extinct. Weather and the availability of food played a major role. The human race can also be wiped out by viruses and disease. Virus mutations can happen at any time in many different environments. In 2014, Africa suffered the worst Ebola Virus outbreak in history. There is no cure for Ebola, and the origin of it has not been completely confirmed. Some scientists' theories believe it came from the bat population and mutated to infect human beings. Ebola has proven that it can mutate. The possibility of it mutating into something even worse is out of our domain of control and reason. It is up to nature.

On the other end of the spectrum, could innovation overcome our wasteful lifestyles? Could new technologies and the expanding clean energy movement help reverse the damage that we have done to the environment? Time will tell, but the facts always prevail. Some scientists say that solar energy harms the environment. Solar energy plants are being built all over the southwest of the United States in the desserts. The open land is seen as prime locations for these solar energy plants. These projects are very massive. Biologists and environmental scientist believe that the solar energy plants disrupt fragile dessert eco systems. They believe that wildlife like the desert tortoises are threatened but there is no definitive proof, although their numbers are steadily declining. Is the eco system for wildlife worth the sacrifice of clean energy? What are our limits? What should we be willing to sacrifice to reverse our own course of environmental demise?

Is our survival more important than that of animals? Technology has put us at the top of the food chain when it comes to decisions that affect eco systems. We have surely abused this power carelessly. But is it all relative? Could it be argued that we have to make mistakes so that we can figure out how to fix things? Or is it ignorant to knowingly make bad choices and be forced to figure out how to make things right again?

Some scientists believe that if we reserve the desertification of the planet that it will it the great equalizer to global warming and pollution. Deserts cover about 50% of the planet, and they are labeled as dry, arid land. More than 2 billion people live in what is considered dry lands and deserts regions. 90% of people that live in dry lands are from developing nations. They also suffer from poor economic and social conditions. The immediate causes of desertification are the removal of vegetation. This includes all kinds of plants. From cutting down trees to animals that eat excess amounts of plants by overgrazing. Vegetation plays the biggest role in determining the biological composition of soil. Soil without diverse nutrients from vegetation becomes barren and dry. Some of the dry soil even gets choked off by a layer of algae that grows over the top of it.

There are techniques that exist to reverse the effects of desertification. One technique that would be useful is contour trenching. What this involves is digging 150m long and 1m deep trenches in the soil. The trenches have to be made parallel to height lines of the landscape so that they prevent the water from flowing and causing erosion. Stone walls are then placed around the trenches to prevent them from closing up again. This method was invented by Peter Westerveld. Implementing these techniques is a major challenge. The obvious first challenge is costs. Who would fund the replenishment of our deserts? Governments or corporations? With our current way of thinking, groups would want to lay claim to any land that they spend money on as if they own it. There is also a lack of political will. Although desertification is one of the biggest threats to biodiversity, not enough important people or groups care about it today.

Is it natural for more awareness to be brought to our environmental issues as our environment gets worse? Because of everything that is going on in the world are we distracted from paying more attention to our surroundings? There is hope that someday society will focus on preventative measures to restoring and protecting our environment. There is also hope that we can recognize the faults in how we use our resources and move forward with alternatives that guarantee longevity.

CONNECTION IGNORED

All of the things that distract us in society leave us disconnected from one another. We have created social groups that tie into whatever fits our comfort zones. Are human beings just naturally creatures of comfort? The clouds of distraction stretch very far, and it seems everyone gets caught up into these clouds. We are more connected to our personal wants and desires .We have even gotten to the point where our own needs are ignored for which we are completely oblivious. It shows in our appearance and even in our health. It also shows in the choices that we make on a daily basis. It's no wonder that the concern for other's rights or well-being is ignored because we cannot see past our own individual needs and wants. We are unwilling to step outside of our groups or comfort zones.

These distractions have taken away our desire for equality, because we are no longer naturally concerned with such things. Equality leads to collective prosperity, for which nothing is greater in this entire world, but it takes a connection minded society to realize this. Inherently, our connection to one another is ignored. The connection isn't ignored because of a direct choice, but because of our environment and the reality and perceptions that we have created. All of the civilized countries in the world live in a bubble. The majority of its citizens have not traveled outside of the countries that they were born in so why should their perceptions on worldly problems or issues have any valid connections?

Third world countries should be a very big concern for any civilized nation. Countries like Sudan and Sierra Leone are plagued by wars and hunger and the lack of education. These types of situations aren't in the interest of civilized countries yet because they don't understand the effects on the world. By letting these things go on will only hurt the entire world. There are 842 million undernourished people in the world today. That means one in eight people do not get enough food to be healthy and lead an active life. Hunger and malnutrition are in fact the number one risk to health worldwide — greater than AIDS, malaria, and tuberculosis combined. The good news is that hunger is entirely solvable. There is enough food in the world to feed everyone and no scientific breakthroughs are needed. Today's knowledge, tools, and policies, combined with political will, can solve the problem. Solving hunger is a "best buy" in today's tough economy. When nations work together to solve hunger and invest in good nutrition, they increase productivity and create economic opportunities. Conversely, studies have shown that countries lose millions of dollars in economic output as a result of child under-nutrition.

According to the most recent estimate that Hunger Notes could find, malnutrition, as measured by stunting, affects 32.5 percent of children in developing countries—one of three (de Onis 2000). Geographically, more than 70 percent of malnourished children live in Asia, 26 percent in Africa and 4 percent in Latin America and the Caribbean. In many cases, their plight began even before birth with a malnourished mother. Under-nutrition among pregnant women in developing countries leads to 1 out of 6 infants born with low birth weight. This is not only a risk factor for neonatal deaths, but also causes learning disabilities, mental retardation, poor health, blindness, and premature death.

The world produces enough food to feed everyone. World agriculture produces 17 percent more calories per person today than it did 30 years ago, despite a 70 percent population increase. This is enough to provide everyone in the world with at least 2,720 kilocalories (kcal) per person per day, according to the most recent estimate that we could find (FAO 2002, p. 9). The principal problem is that many people in the world do not have sufficient land to grow, or income to purchase, enough food.

3.1 percent of the world's population is hungry. That's roughly 925 million people who go undernourished on a daily basis, consuming less than the recommended 2,100 calories a day. The world produces enough food to feed all 7 billion people who live in it, but those who go hungry either do not have land to grow food or money to purchase it. The difference between hunger and malnutrition is that malnutrition means the body does not have the necessary vitamins and nutrients necessary to grow or fight off disease. In developing countries where sanitation is poor, lack of nutrition only makes children and adults more vulnerable to illness. Poverty is the main cause of hunger, and hunger is a cause of poverty. When people go malnourished, they lose brain functionality and the mental resources to be a productive asset in society or earn money. In 2010, an estimated 7.6 million children — more than 20,000 a day — died from hunger. Nearly 98 percent of worldwide hunger exists in underdeveloped countries. Hunger is often passed from mother to child. Each year, 17 million children are born underweight because their mothers are malnourished. Almost 1 in every 15 children in developing countries dies from hunger. While hunger exists worldwide, 62.4 percent of the hunger exists in Asia/South Pacific. .

More than 20 percent of children in Asia and Africa are underweight for their age. When a mother is undernourished during pregnancy, the baby is often born undernourished, too. Every year, 17 million children are born this way due to a mother's lack of nutrition before and during pregnancy. Similarly, women in hunger are so deficient of basic nutrients (like iron) that 315,000 die during childbirth from hemorrhaging every year. The number of undernourished people decreased nearly 30 percent in Asia and the Pacific, from 739 million to 563 million, largely due to socio-economic progress in many countries in the region. The prevalence of undernourishment in the region decreased from 23.7 percent to 13.9 percent. Hunger is also a cause of poverty, and thus of hunger. By causing poor health, low levels of energy, and even mental impairment, hunger can lead to even greater poverty by reducing people's ability to work and learn, thus leading to even greater hunger. Using the new estimates, there were 1 billion hungry people in 1990-92, and the world population was 5,370 million (US census estimates for 1991). Thus the proportion was .18 and halving it would be .09. The current proportion (870 million hungry divided by 2013 world population of 7,095) is .123. Thus in 2013, the world is .033 away, or 234 million people, from reaching this target.

Harmful economic systems are the principal cause of poverty and hunger. Hunger Notes believes that the principal underlying cause of poverty and hunger is the ordinary operation of the economic and political systems in the world. Essentially, control over resources and income is based on military, political, and economic power that typically ends up in the hands of a minority, who live well, while those at the bottom barely survive, if they do. We have described the operation of this system in more detail in our special section on harmful economic systems.

Environmental factors, land degradation and the deforestation of lands, often by big businesses, are a cause of hunger. As lands are clear-cut for cattle ranching or farms, they are left unprotected from wind and water erosion. In addition, economic pressures force many farmers to adopt farming practices which meet short-term needs but cause long-term damage to the environment. This results in unsustainable farming techniques that often ruin land for future use. This results in land that produces fewer or no crops and is more vulnerable to erosion in the event of drought, floods, or heavy winds.

Solving hunger is also a contribution to peace and stability. When governments can no longer guarantee adequate food supplies, states are prone to fall. Volatility on food markets can quickly translate into volatility on the streets. Finally, solving hunger lays the foundation for progress in many other areas of development, including health and education. Well-nourished women have healthier, heavier babies whose immune systems are stronger for life. A healthy, well-fed child is also more likely to attend school. Good progress was made in reducing chronic hunger in the 1980s and the 1990s, but progress began to level off between 2000 and 2010. All of us – citizens, employers, corporate leaders, and governments – must work together to end hunger.

Across the globe, conflicts consistently disrupt farming and food production. Fighting also forces millions of people to flee their homes, leading to hunger emergencies as the displaced find themselves without the means to feed themselves. The conflict in Syria is a recent example. People living in poverty cannot afford nutritious food for themselves and their families. This makes them weaker and less able to earn the money that would help them escape poverty and hunger. This is not just a day-to-day problem: when children are chronically malnourished, or "stunted," it can affect their future income, condemning them to a life of poverty and hunger.

In addition to local elites and governments changing the rules in the past, globalization in the modern era is seeing another assault on local communities' lands. A number of countries are buying up or securing deals with poorer countries to use their land. But this use is not for helping the poor country with their food security issues. Instead it is to ensure food security for the investor country, or it is for the investor's own commercial benefit.

DIVIDED WE STAND

WE STAND DIVIDED IN OPINIONS, BECAUSE PEOPLE feel that an opinion is their identity and their freedom. There is absolutely nothing wrong with opinion, but if there is no willingness to meet a common ground when opinions clash that's where we have problems. Opinions are based off of individual perception and conclusions. We all perceive the world and ourselves and every subject matter differently. Wouldn't it be a more logical thing to bring our perceptions together to combine collectively with those of others? We also stand divided in our religions and ideologies, but this would not be so bad if there was more acceptance and understanding in the world. The history of culture and religion is ignored because our minds seek conflict. We seek our own conflict resolutions before we attempt to understand different situations. This is why racial issues divide us because of our primitive comparisons to one another.

We let the color of someone's skin be the determining factor of what you expect from them or how they should be treated. This is comparable to prehistoric thinking and is the exact opposite of educated or civilized. Some people believe that this type of thinking and segregation should be made illegal. All of our time and energy spent on racial issues throughout the years is one of the most distracting things from progress that we have ever faced. Race is a factor in jobs, politics, education, and even personal advancement. The issue with race needs to be abolished because we are one race. We are all human and all equal. We are all capable of the same things. The only thing that separates us is our likes and dislikes and talents. If we cannot see past these completely primitive issues then we are collectively lost.

Racism has been used as a device to continue to divide the United States. Very often it is talked about in the news to incite hatred and continue to divide the populace. It has been here since before slavery and even before the United States was formed. It is one of the tools used by government and media to divide and conquer. Year after year everyone falls for it and picks a side. Celebrating black history month every year isn't really effective in fighting racism. Black History is part of American history and should be taught as such. Singling out black history in America as if it was the worst thing that happened in American history is a bit extreme. Black history is very important, but segregating it from the rest of American history gives the wrong message. No other heritage group has been given an entire month or holiday that is even comparable to black history month. There is no Native American History month. The Native Americans were not slaves, but their history could arguably be comparable or much worse than black history. There is no Jewish History month. The Holocaust was arguably one of the most cruel and extreme things to ever happen to any group in the last 1,000 years.

Why don't we have segregated months or holidays for any other groups that bad things happened to? There is a reason why black history month exists and it's not to actually celebrate black history. Black history month exists as a form of psychological war-fare to constantly remind the black community every year that racism exists. This type of constant reminder instills a victim mentality that breeds for generations. This victim mentality influences the black community to believe that there is something against them before anything has even happened in most cases. Expecting someone to treat you a certain way because you are a different race influences many different types of self-segregation. You can walk into many different schools or neighborhoods and look at kids' social interactions. Most kids only associate with their own race or social group that they are comfortable with. It is a very high chance that black students will only associate with other black students because of this. This type of self-segregating mentality leads to a lot of racial misunderstandings. These misunderstandings and segregations filter up into adulthood and to many different walks of life. It affects jobs for the black community in a heavy way. White managers and executives in the corporate world that have never worked with black people, or rarely interacted with black people, are less likely to be diverse when it comes to hiring practices or interactions. It does not necessarily mean that they are racist but it demonstrates that people operate within their own comfort zones and only understand what they are exposed to. We have to break this cycle. Not just for blacks but for every community of people. We have to proactively seek to understand. But how would someone be motivated to step outside of their comfort zone? This can only be accomplished in a person's upbringing. Parents don't do a good enough job of this, because by the time they have children they are already living in a comfort zone of their own.

Some people believe that they see racism in their daily lives only because they believe in racism. If they have experienced racism in the past then they automatically assume it is happening again after being treated a certain way. It could be repeated racism, but sometimes people overlook the fact that not everyone is nice. Bad treatment could be motivated by a lot of different things other than racism. There is a saying that misery loves company. A lot of viewpoints and perceptions are flawed simply because of the belief in racism. This also feeds the viewpoints and perception of white privilege. Believing that something is wrong with your race or that you have it harder than another race actually is a defeating mechanism on a psychological level. Some people respond to it positively while some people just seemingly give up on life and never strive for anything greater.

We are also divided on opinions of the gay community. Most of it comes from religious beliefs. How can you hold someone responsible for acting or living a certain way if they do not believe in your religion? Religion is also used as a tool of segregation when it encounters certain lifestyles that do not fit the mold of rules set forth by it. None of this is even logical. There are many different religions in the world, and there are also people that don't believe in any religion at all. It doesn't have to mean that we are divided, but that is how we interpret difference. Diversity should be welcomed and respected, but logic doesn't always prevail. Almost every religious group claims to be the correct religion and the only religion someone can believe in if they are to receive salvation or an afterlife. This is also the reason for religious division. There are so many different religions, so people stay in the comfort zones of the religion that they are taught.

Each new generation seems to get a little bit better when it comes to working together and social problems such as race and religion. We are slowly starting to see the foolishness of our ways. We see it with the legalization of gay marriage, but it is not completely legal everywhere. In some countries people are still executed for being gay. People are also still being executed for being of a different religious group. In August of

2014 the Yezidi people of Iraq were being slaughtered by extremist Muslims for refusing to convert. To modern logic and thinking this is absolutely primitive and a direct violation of basic human rights. We are fighting against a culture that believes in killing anyone that is not the same as them. Violence erupts when different religious groups burn each other's holy books. They fight as if someone has burned the last and only book of their religion and all is lost. This is madness and sad that anyone is offended to the point of erupting violence.

Everything that divides us is passed down through generations. But it is our choice to continue down the path of certain traditions or listen to what we are taught by generations before us. There is no requirement to continue old ways of thinking. We are supposed to evolve past the old ways and invent new ways of thinking. If our thinking doesn't evolve, then how could we ever come together? Could we naturally be torn apart in these issues? Is it human nature to find difference in others and hold it against them? Is it human nature to want to feel different or superior to certain groups of people? Regardless of nature, it is a choice even if you make the choice without knowing.

On November 9th 1989 the Berlin Wall fell. It was one of the biggest symbols of communist oppression in Europe. At the end of World War 2, Berlin was completely destroyed because of Nazism. The winners of the war divided Germany up. The Soviet Union occupied and controlled East Germany with hopes that a socialism system would show the world how a country should prosper. West Germany would be occupied by America, Britain, and France. West Germany was democratic and would be in direct opposition to the socialist communism of East Germany. This created big complications because Berlin was in the middle of Eastern Communist controlled Germany. Half of Berlin would be a non-communist island within a communist nation. Many people that lived in East Germany migrated to the West because of communism. Many of them did it by simply crossing the border that was set in Berlin.

By 1961 many of the people that live in East Berlin had migrated to West Berlin. Over 2 and a half million people moved away from the communist East Berlin from 1945 to 1961. They did not like the lack of free speech and political freedom that resided under Communism so they made it clear by just walking over the border. During this time it was estimated that every 3 minutes one person left East Germany and relocated to the West. The continued loss of labor workers threaten the survival of East Germany. The communist party of East Berlin decided to build a wall to make it harder for people to leave. This caused many families to be split. It even caused people that worked in West Berlin but lived the East to lose their jobs. West Berlin became isolated and segregated. People in West Berlin protested the wall and even blamed the United States for not getting involved.

This conflict is part of our human history in terms of segregation. Governments and groups wanting to build walls to control the populace instead of fixing what is wrong with the government. Instead of taking the time to understand why the population of East Berlin wasn't happy there they would rather control them with a wall. This is very similar to what is happening today in America. The wall that is being built is more of a metaphor but the ideas portrayed to us through the media and the government create walls in our thinking. Certain demographic groups of people are portrayed a certain way in movies and in how news is reported. We develop psychological expectations based off of what we see on T.V. These expectations are sometimes flawed but they are intentional. It is easier to control a group of people that is misinformed or divided. Division has become one of the main talking points on the news. No one agrees much on many different subjects, whether it be politics or religion. The news does conduct themed interviews showing people arguing and sometimes even screaming at each other. This type of mentality aside from whatever subject matter they disagree on filters down into the way we interact with each other.

There is a saying that says lead by example. Well, we are following that example in all walks of life. In our marriages, our jobs, and many different areas in life. There is an underlying theme of conflict that has infected everyone. Do we really have control of our minds if we can be so easily influenced into conflict? Most of the time people don't even know why they are disagreeing with one another or why they dislike something someone is saying or expressing. Conflict without knowing the root cause or even caring about the root cause is very ridiculous. There is also no desire to solve the conflict or argument, which leads to bigger conflicts until no one even remembers why it started.

There is something called Conflict Theory, and it is a way of studying the inequality of different groups in society. It is based on the ideas of Karl Marx in the 19th century. He believed that society evolves through several different stages. Those 3 stages were Feudalism, Capitalism, and Socialism. For example, 19th century Europe was a Capitalist Society. The rich upper class of Europe were called the Bourgeoisie, and they were the minority of the population. The poor lower class of Europe were the Proletariat. The Proletariat made up the majority of the population. You would think that the majority of the population would have more power or sway than the minority, but this was not the case. The Bourgeoisie were in control. They even owned all of the factories and stores that produced all of the food that people needed. The Bourgeoisie sold what they produced to make a living. The Proletariat depended on their labor in the factories to make a living, and they depended on the Bourgeoisie to get paid. This clearly wasn't a one sided dependency. Each side was dependent on one another to make progress.

The Bourgeoisie would never admit this because they didn't want to lose any of their power over the Proletariat majority. The economic inequality was obvious and would most likely fuel a change in society. The working class realized that they were being exploited, and it lead to them uniting and creating a class support group. A society where one group exploits another group economically would be setting the foundation for its own destruction. In a Capitalist society the accepted thesis was that the Bourgeoisie was in control and the working class did all of the labor. The desire of the working class to change the way things were would be the definition of an antithesis. A thesis and antithesis cannot exist together peacefully in a democratic society. One side is not happy with the way things are and the other side is happy with the way things are. This creates conflict and is also an example of the way things are today in America. The struggle between both sides might eventually lead to a compromise or a synthesis of both sides.

They could resolve the tensions between both sides by creating a new outlook. They would give members of the working class higher positions in society to seemingly make them feel better about the capitalist situation. The combination of the thesis and antithesis would result in a new class of people, the middle class. This middle class would have more influence than the minority Bourgeoisie because there would be more of them. But the antithesis can derive from any source of unrest to oppose the thesis. The lower labor class could develop resentment towards the middle class or the upper rich class could feel threatened by the middle class. Both of these would be a new antithesis to the original thesis and cause a whole new conflict all over again while the cycle continues. The society that we live in is very complex and not even Conflict Theory can completely explain why there are times of stability and times of seemingly great resolution. Conflicts have the ability to spring up anywhere about any subject and are not only unique to working class conflicts or disagreements. We all have different perspectives simply because we all come from different walks of life. Root cause of conflicts can all be a result of a correct viewpoint. But the viewpoint only applies to the person experiencing something that has created their view. With so many conflicts, who is right and who is wrong? Could it be possible that no one is completely right and no one is completely wrong in their recognition of a conflict? The solution would be some kind of conflict resolution, but that is impossible if you don't know why there is conflict or where it came from. Our conflicts with Race, Religion, and Politics are constantly ongoing. Every week, every month, and every year there is a major event that touches on these subject matters. These conflicts are used against us to divide us. History continually repeats itself and those in control purposely do this as if they are guiding the conflict in their favor. If the population is focused on conflicts that don't really matter then the government can more easily control what kind of laws are being passed. They can control what kind of policies are being made. Year after year, more and more rights are being taken away from us while we focus on things that divide us.

We stand divided and proud. We believe we are patriotic and walk with our heads high. We believe that we live in freedom. There is a difference between a man that thinks he is free and a man that feels his freedom. Our society needs to wake up and realize that the conflicts for which we spend so much time on are not in our best interest. We stand divided but we will never be free until we are united.

ENLIGHTENED

We look for purpose in life because we have strayed away from our natural balance of thought. We've let all the created segregations completely sever our connections. Our purpose was to always take care of one another to the fullest extent. These days the purpose of creating things is directly tied to profit or the expectation in return that benefits the individual instead of who finds use of what is created. Money has been the biggest divider of all of us. If money is the root of all evil, then there is no evil greater than segregation of culture, class, sex, and religion. This is exactly what money has done to us. Money has taken us down the path of divide and conquer since our inception and invention of material value. We've lost our identity and uniqueness. The meaning of uniqueness has been individualized and turned into a personal attribute. We are all one, which makes us unique. Not as individuals, but holistically as a species.

We have to ask ourselves what our ultimate purpose is. Is our ultimate purpose to continue a pursuit of manufactured happiness and pleasure? Or is our purpose what we make it? One road leads to a continuation of the way things are until a collective demise encumbers us all. The other road of true purpose and change in the interest not of self-serving endeavors leads to collective prosperity. The choice of this path lies in the hands of us all. It is not the responsibility of government or corporations to drive or influence this change. We have always had this power, but it is not exercised because not enough believe in this power. The truth is we have always had the power.

Enlightenment is when you get to a point in life where one seeks to understand instead of judging. Manufactured differences like Political affiliations, Religion, Race, or Sexual Orientation are ignored. Seeing through the clouds of difference breaks the chains of ignorance which leads to categorized hatred and discrimination. Once these mental barriers fall it leads to an enlightened path. A path that sees no limits in potential not just individually but collectively. In every walk of life togetherness is needed. Through technology, innovation, and discovery we all depend on each other for some type of support. That support comes in all forms and categories, and it connects us all together. With enlightened minds we even see one another more clearly. We appreciate and value the lives of our fellow man through diversity and understanding.

We are creatures of comfort, but we must have the strength to break free of comfort and not allow our world to be ruled by emotions that blind the sight of our hearts. The truth is as adults we lost something that we once had as children. The ability to forgive, forget, and smile was much easier back then. I think as adults we can look to children to teach us how we should treat one another. That innocence uncorrupted by our selfish system that tears us apart. Knowing that the path we are on leads us to nowhere can only be made aware through drastic change in thought. Understanding each other without opinion or motive without the intention of superiority is part of an enlightened path.

But first we have to re-connect with ourselves. How can we truly connect with one another if we don't know ourselves or love ourselves? The battle to be enlightened starts inside all of us first. To know your fellow man is to truly know yourself.

QUOTES AND SAYINGS, M. REINBERG

THOUGHTS ON CIVIL RIGHTS-

"After watching the news on August 19th, 2014 someone asked me how do we (Black People) fight racism? Do you believe marching and protesting helps? I really thought about the question. How should we fight racism? Didn't they already march for our civil rights? Didn't our forefathers already suffer worse atrocities so that we can vote? So that we were allowed to get an education and jobs? Didn't our forefathers set the stage for us already? Then I began to ask myself: Why are my people still marching instead of educating themselves? Why are we killing each other more than other races kill us? Do you think Martin Luther King sacrificed his time and his life so that we could grow up to be rappers, and womanize? And walk out on our families? Did Rosa Parks refuse to move to the back of the bus so that we live in a backwards mentality? Our ancestors sacrificed their lives so that we could be Doctors, Lawyers, Business Men/Women, and Community Organizers. Not just for the Black race, but to be living examples for every race of people. To show by our actions and opportunities that no matter how low you are or how low you feel nothing can stop you from flying. So I will fight racism by loving my neighbor, even those that hate me. I will fight racism by giving no response to the ignorant. I will fight racism by constantly growing in body and mind through education and fitness. I will fight racism by inventing and innovating. I will fight racism by being the exact opposite of stereotypes to the point where anyone who is ignorant enough to be racist towards me is comparative to primitive cave men. This is how we fight racism. Not by marching and protesting, but by giving society no choice but to recognize your value because of an overwhelming positive contribution to it."

THOUGHTS ON LIFE-

"I sit in deep thought a lot. Thinking about history. The world. My own life. My friends and loved ones. I sit and I wonder. I wonder what the point of everything is. What is the purpose? How do we define ourselves? Down to the core of our species. The barriers that separate us all from one another are of our own creation. Politics, Religion, Race, Sexual Orientation, Rich, Poor. Why do we do this? Do we misunderstand a lost desire that sleeps inside of all of us? A desire to feel special, or important, or have purpose? Is this desire twisted to serve individualism? Is it because we ignore our true connections to one another? We don't have to prosper as individuals. We are all pioneers. In every facet of life. All of our combined experiences, cultures, intellect, motivations, and even failures. There is something to be learned from everyone that has ever existed. We are part of something that is bigger than any one category of assumed definition of life's origin. We are one. Unified even while these barriers currently exist. Continue down the path of life that builds walls and barriers at your own risk. Upon the end of your life when you are taking those last breaths you will realize that you did not truly live a life at all."

OUR LOSSES ARE OUR GAINS-

"We know loss. The reality check of mortality gives us subtle reminders of our own fates. Sadness, Regret, and Despair fill us with sorrow. Our hearts become hardened and numb. Such is life. That darkness that tells us to give up. To lose hope. To let the memories of what we once had haunt our remaining days. Like fireworks, our fuses are lit and then we burn out. All fires eventually burn out; it is guaranteed. But even so, we have a choice to pick up our broken hearts. To turn our losses into gains. To turn our excuses into opportunities. We have the choice to grow. Never forgetting where we came from because it is what made us. Do you see the light? It is there when you look in the mirror. It is you. The light is all of us. Join me inside of it."

WHAT IS THIS LIFE FOR?

"Why are we alive? Why do we participate in things that stop us from becoming closer as human beings? What is the point of knowingly hindering the progression of the entire human race? Why do we care more about our short lives or individual problems more than the lives that we affect in the future and all around us? How can we define ourselves as intelligent if all we do is find ways to segregate ourselves from one another instead of coming together without any regard to opinions and beliefs? Why do we reserve love for our families or friends or children? Why don't we look at strangers with the same love and respect that is sacredly reserved for those closest to us? Love transcends everything. It is the most powerful expression that we possess. This life is meant for that and love is meant for everyone."

EXPECTATIONS FULFILMENT-

"We base our needs off of the expectations we place on others. Fulfilment becomes impossible. We grow more miserable as our expectations are never met. Why do we torture ourselves so? Fulfilment has nothing to do with other people. We lose ourselves to this thought process, never to recover. An empty shell, and glass with a hole. We bleed until we die. But Fulfilment comes from inside of us. What we don't realize is that the glass is already full and never loses its contents."

WE ARE MOUNTAINS-

"Sometimes people think they are screwing you over, adding stress to your life, and taking advantage of you. They may even deceive you and hide things from you. You have the wings to fly above it all. You cannot be moved. You are a Mountain. Only God moves mountains."

EVER SO SINGLE RELATIONSHIPS-

"If you are single don't sweat it. Spend time working on yourself. Travel and go to the gym. Spend time with friends and family. Make great moments count. You have to live life one stage at a time and enjoy it all. Don't let what you want blind you to what you have. Losing your identity to chase relationships will never make you happy. Don't become an empty cup."

EMOTIONAL SICKNESS-

"Our emotional state and level of stress directly affect our health. If you get sick a lot, it may not be germs. So think about your life and get rid of as much negativity as possible."

THAT MILITARY VETERAN-

"When a Military Veteran tells you he misses being deployed or going to war, don't mistake him/her for having an itch for violence and killing. What that veteran misses is something that society doesn't have. That is comradery. What is wrong with the world that we have to go to war to feel like someone has our back or that we are supported and that someone would die so that you get home safe?"

TURN THINGS AROUND-

"Bad things happen to good people all the time. But good people find a way to turn things around. There is nothing good about giving up or letting bad things overtake you."

OPINIONS DON'T MATTER-

"In life, one of the greatest feelings is doing what people said you couldn't."

COURAGE AND COWARDS-

"Sometimes it takes courage to take responsibility, but cowards will focus on placing blame."

GUN CONTROL OR CULTURAL CONSEQUENCE?

"If someone has made the decision to kill they will use whatever type of weapons that are available. Let's think about gun control for a second. Sure, take guns away. I can still use my car to run people down. Knives, crossbows, homemade projectiles, the list goes on. The problem is not guns but our inability to take responsibility for the world and culture of violence that we have created."

MY VALUES CHANGE-

"As a kid I used to dream about having a car and a house. All I dream of now is a world without hunger and war. A world with a cross-cultural collaboration that has never been seen. I guess this means I know what is really important in life. We are born naked with nothing and die the same. All that matters is what we do between the beginning and the end, because all we take with us is our legacy."

SURVIVAL-

"The Universe does not care about our survival. 99% of all species that have ever lived on this planet are extinct. Our survival depends on the choices we make against the nature of all things ending."

DRONES OF WAR-

"When we outsource our wars to machines we are no longer connected to humanity."

OULOOK-

"When you train your mind to focus on the good things amidst the bad, you have conquered life. Suffering creates resilience. Failure gives you experience. All challenges are relative. Each one leads to a new challenge. We are ever growing."

TECHNOLOGY AND SOCIAL MEDIA

WITH SOCIAL MEDIA AND TECHNOLOGY ADVANCING, it gives us more opportunity for vital news, and keeps us more aware than ever with what is going on around the world. Social networks like Twitter, Facebook, and Myspace have connected us in a way that was not part of our world a generation ago. But have these new forms of communication hindered our ability to communicate in other ways and keep in touch in person rather than over the Internet? There used to be a time where friends would grow up together, graduate high school, and move away to college. Those friends would probably lose contact with one another as their lives grew and changed. But the true friends that never lost contact no matter what life threw at them almost no longer exist. They don't exist as they once did because everyone that we call friend has an opportunity to just follow you on Twitter or Facebook and never miss a beat. They can stay updated on your life just with a single click of the mouse with absolutely no personal interaction required. There is no need to ask questions or call your friends anymore to see how they are doing. Inquiring friends can just scroll through an endless archive of news feeds, status updates, and pictures. This is not a bad thing, but it does take out a very special element of what true friendship communication used to be. Is this something that we should worry about? Has this form of social media connection dissolved a very important element in our relationships that we cherish?

Social media and technology seem to be replacing human interaction in our society. Face to face communication is ultimately fading away because of all the new social technologies. Researchers have been studying this phenomenon for the past decade and are extremely intrigued by it. Social competency is something that mostly everyone strives for. It has become a very important ideal in society. But there is a lot of evidence that shows social media does more harm than good. For example, a study executed by the National Institutes of Health found that youths with strong, positive face-to-face relationships may be those most frequently using social media as an additional venue to interact with their peers. According to Forbes magazine, only 7% of communication is based on the verbal word. This obviously means that over 90% of communication is based on social media. Facebook hurts relationships more than it helps, because it does not promote two-way communication. It is easier to post a generic comment on Facebook, with no real feedback, than it is to compose a personal email that will probably get feedback. Because of the number of people viewing the information, the information cannot be specific. For safety, all information has to be general.

It falls right in line with the ongoing debate over the social impact of social media. At the center of the argument is whether technology is causing us to sacrifice social connections for digital and virtual ones. Americans have become much more socially isolated and have fewer connections with their neighbors and communities, which led researchers to speculate that one cause may be the dramatic rise in Internet usage and mobile devices over the last twenty years.

A common tech etiquette downfall is never disconnecting.

Does the thought of being stuck with a dead phone battery make your heart race? Does forgetting your phone send you into a panic? When your phone buzzes, do you have a compulsion to respond immediately at any cost? Or maybe you've experienced "phantom vibration syndrome," a term coined for those who experience that common false alarm phone vibration. If all this sounds familiar, then this can describe anyone.

Overuse with your smartphones and social networking activities may actually hinder your relationships. "Technology is making us more social and helping us to connect, but we have to use good judgment. We are very reliant on our technology. That's not a bad thing. It helps us become more available and recognizable, which helps bring us more business. But we need to know when to use it, when to turn it off, and how to use it appropriately."

With the invention of technologies that are able to overcome the obstacles of time and space, one would think that these tools would be used to gain an understanding of other cultures, meet people all over the world, maintain and strengthen familial relationships, communicate effectively with others, and help people to become more socially adept. However, some technological advances cause people to be distracted, overly stressed, and increasingly isolated. Many people are involved in an abundant number of relationships through technology, but sometimes the quantity of these associations leaves people feeling qualitatively empty. Obviously, technology has had a profound impact on what it means to be social.

OUR MONETARY SYSTEMS AND HUMAN ADVANCEMENT

THE REAL POWER IN THIS WORLD LIES IN THE HANDS and influence of corporate giants in the global financial market. But this form of power has to be an expected inevitability of our own created monetary system. Money is the ultimate power. The more money you have, the more powerful you are. Having a profitable organization equates to success in finance but at some point, success turns into greed and control. The concept of money or currency was to give a person's work some type of value. Money is also a huge limitation that we have placed on ourselves. Organizations like NASA or medical research programs all around the world are limited by funding. If these types of organizations that obviously benefit all of us were not limited by money, how much more advanced would we be? How much farther could our ambitious minds reach into space? How many more diseases would we cure? The potential is unlimited but since there is not monetary profit directly connected to the benefits, we let its growth be limited by money.

Money limits the potential of everything. Ideas and innovations that don't receive funding are dead because of our own created concepts. Some may put this in the category of competition or the natural order of our monetary system, but it falls in the realm of created limitation. True prosperity is absent of any types of limits. The state of the world today and our monetary system has given all of that prosperity to profits. A profit is nothing but a delusion of what success really is. With profit you can buy things or influence people, but profit is not tangible. Profit doesn't invent or think of new ways to do things. Profit in itself is empty.

The entire model of our lifestyle is based off of profit. We are taught to go to school and gain higher education so that we have the opportunity to make more money so that we prosper. But money has simply taken over everything. The biggest infection of a system that is corrupted by our monetary system in America is Prisons and our horribly broken judicial system. There is a new wave of For-Profit Prisons that give donations to politicians who pass bills that give government money to the private prison industry. The private prisons even get money if their prisons are not full or housing enough inmates. The sad thing about this entire situation is that it corrupts our judicial process. If private prisons are quoting the government for services, then the government is forced to convict more people so that they can fill these prisons and get their money's worth. This is a very unethical practice, and it affects the rights of the United States citizens. When the judicial system is faced with inmate quotas because of government money spent on private prisons, then it cannot be expected that every person that breaks the law is getting a fair sentence for whatever crime they are guilty of.

The people that run these private prisons only care about profit. The government doesn't want to build more prisons so this is seen as an alternate to save money.

Of all the problems we face in the world today, most of them cost money to solve. Billions of dollars have been poured into research for diseases of which we have not yet found a cure for. Cancer and AIDS are 2 of the biggest ones. Why would we let something as fickle as money, for which we are the creators, limit the amount of research done that would lead to a possible cure? If we have the power to create money, wealth, and debt; then why don't we have the power to bypass our own monetary system for things that are arguably more important than anything else? The value of life ties directly to the cost of health. Life is not something that can be purchased, so why would health or quality of it be an exception? None of us asked for life, so there should be a fierce reliability of health endeavors not limited by the clutches of money. This isn't just an issue of curing diseases. Treatment for diseases has become all too common of a goal.

Since the year 2001 the total cost of war just in Afghanistan is over 700 billion dollars. The cost of war in Iraq since the year 2003 is over 800 billion dollars. Both of these figures continue to rise every day. The total cost of both wars will reach over 1.6 trillion dollars and continue to go higher and higher as long as we keep fighting with no true end goal. It can be argued that keeping a presence in both countries is borderline occupation and continues the cycle, ensuring that there is always conflict. This is very beneficial to government contracting companies that also get paid by United States tax revenue. This bleeds money away that could be used for education or science.

Treating diseases has turned into a huge industry of profit. Not enough money is focused towards cures, so the next best thing is treatment. Big pharmaceutical companies are profit driven. They may argue that they are doing a service to society by treating many things with their drugs. But how much of their profit goes towards curing something they are treating? They just invent better and more potent drugs over time that fall very short of cures. It can be argued that treating different diseases or conditions is better than nothing at all, but are we really satisfied with that?

Scientific advancements are also hindered by our Monetary System. Space exploration and research depends on how much money the government is willing to commit to these programs. But the truth of the matter is that it should be one of the most important things to our society aside from curing diseases. It is very naïve to believe that someday we will not eventually outgrow our own planet with our rate of population growth and resource consumption. Instead we spend over 60% of our budget on government and national security. We only spend 3% of our total budget on Scientific Research and programs. A logical future-minded person would agree that this is not responsible. Also, only 6% of our budget goes to education. This is not beneficial to the generations that will inherit what we leave behind. This is a digression in advancement. We need inventors, engineers, and scientists for the future, and investing in it is our best chance of sustainability. Sadly, the mindset of today's generation thinks profit is the best way of sustainability.

In 2013 a study showed that nearly 1 in 5 scientists in the United States are leaving the United States or considering leaving because of Federal funding cuts to science. This is a very bad situation, because our infrastructure needs scientists to continue. A lot of scientific research is outsourced to other countries because of our lack of scientists already. Government decisions to cut the funding of scientific programs and research negatively impacts the dreams of generations. In a society where innovation has not much influence it should be a crime to not fund our best programs. In 2013 and 2014 the NASA budget was cut twice. We went to the moon in the 1960s but have not sent men anywhere farther than that in over 40 years. This is a sad reality and also a good example of the limitations that money puts on innovation.

We have the resources and technology to send people to Mars and beyond to other planets. But we don't do it simply because of money and funding. Is this really logical? We are held back by a currency that is only given value by us. If we consider ourselves an intelligent life form, then we also have to consider that the concept of our monetary system is very primitive. We have outgrown the constraints of money. Technology, research, and advancement that would benefit the entire world have to be considered a priceless endeavor. These endeavors should be immune to the idea of monetary restraints. But instead, most of the ideas of our best scientists sit on the drawing board. They wait and hope that government or private investors are interested enough to fund their research. Because of budget cuts, some of the space industry has been privatized. Companies like Space-X for example launch satellites and do their own space research. These private companies are also in competition to build the next manned space-craft for NASA.

Is it smart that the space industry has been privatized? This is exactly the problem with having a monetary system involved in innovation. A private company builds something for the government, but then it charges the government fees to use it? This is no different than any business model for anything. There cannot be an expectation of the best if there is a price tag attached. Everything they develop will abide by the constraints of money. The best product will be based off of the best they can do with the money that they have available for whatever they are producing. This is a constraint.

How did it ever come to this? It was driven by major capitalism initiatives after the United States Great Depression in October of 1929. In current day, banks are making some of the same mistakes that lead to the economic collapse of the

Great Depression. When everything becomes about profit and then a downfall isn't far behind. Greed will always lead to demise.

Maybe if we did not have so many enemies we would be able to focus our money in places that wouldn't only temporarily impact our society in a positive way. There needs to be a new vision for our country and for the world. There also needs to be a new vision for the future and what we leave behind. Our current path is not sustainable and eventually leads to catastrophic failure wrapped in good intentions. The rate for which we consume food and energy only increases every year. As our population grows and resources are consumed, we will eventually outgrow this planet. At the point that we can no longer sustain the world in its current state, money will no longer matter. It is possible that future wars will be driven by absolute control of resources if we do not find more viable energy and food alternatives.

What is our goal as a society? Is it to constantly repeat mistakes of the past and call it a different name? Is it to be slaves to our own limited monetary system? I believe that we were meant for much greater things. We are capable of much greater things. Human potential is unlimited. We can manifest almost anything that we imagine. Why would we limit our dreams or potential with money? How many great ideas fail because of funding? How many people without money miss out on the opportunity to make history because of money? Our monetary system is the enemy to true human potential. It is obvious that our potential has no limits. But there are chains on our future. These chains are in our pockets and our bank accounts. We want these chains and strive to have more of it no matter how successful or rich we become. What we want is not tangible and it is not real. Just like life money is only temporary. It is temporary because our

CONNECTION LOST

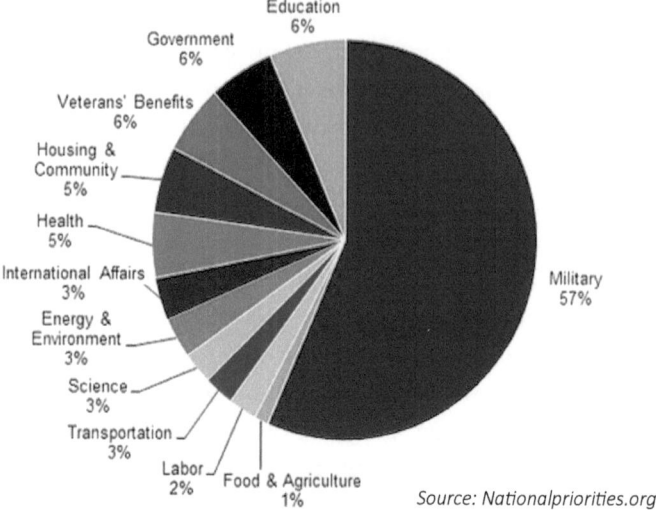

Source: Nationalpriorities.org

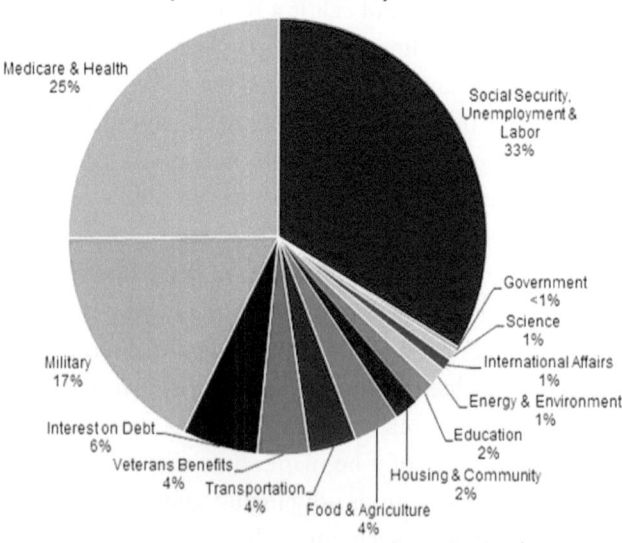

Source: Nationalpriorities.org

lives are temporary. Human advancement is not temporary. It is passed down through generations and it also evolves into better things. The ideas of science sadly meet the grim reality of funding and bureaucracy.

Have you ever thought of what the world would be like if there were no limitations based on money? What would college and higher education be like if everyone in every country had the ability to gain higher education for free? Would there be poverty if every person was provided food for free? These 2 things are within our capabilities even in our current monetary system of capitalism. If people didn't have to think about paying their bills or feeding their families, then our minds would be able to focus and I believe we would be smarter. How long would technology advance keep speeding up? Attempting to predict where technology may take us in future, and how quickly we will get there, is fun and challenging to think about. A lot of the science

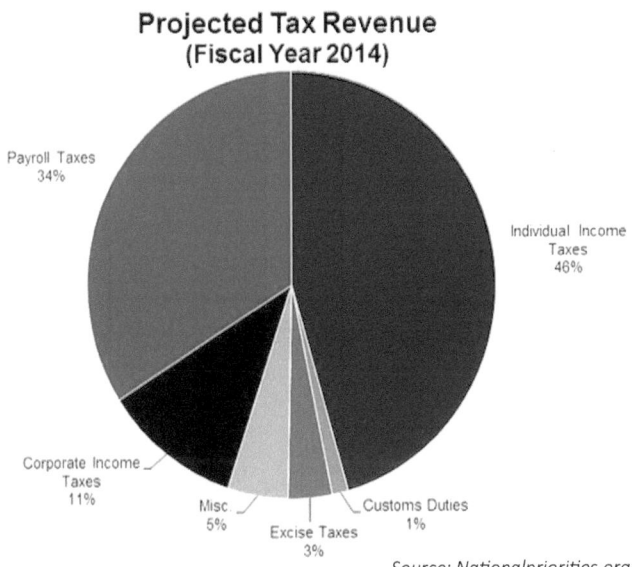

Source: Nationalpriorities.org

fiction sounding ideas people have come up with are exciting, but can we expect to see progress much more rapid than was seen with the invention of radio, for example? As much as we would like to think technological progress is increasing exponentially and that new inventions will appear more and more quickly in hopes they will save our eco system, it is unlikely to happen like that. While scientific progress will continue, the human limitations around how quickly we can learn and how quickly we are willing to adopt new ideas will ensure that our advancement will not be truly exponential.

In the face of overpopulation and resulting problems, technology is very unlikely to save the day. The very rate at which new technologies can achieve market penetration will be limited by the rate at which we can learn about them. The adoption of new ideas doesn't happen overnight even when the information is readily available. One of our biggest problems is that we are already overloaded with too much information. Information is often contradictory and has highly varying quality. Deciding what to believe is sometimes difficult. Critical thinking skills are needed to assess the information and decide what to take or record and what to get rid of. What seems like exponential growth to us now is actually a variable rate of change that will decline again until some new technology comes along to increase the rate at which we can decipher and obtain information. The leading factor will be how much information we can handle as humans beings. But we should expect basic human limitations to change radically or rapidly, as changes are unlikely to be noticeable within a human lifetime.

The current rapid rate of advancement and technological development is probably due to electronic mass media. It can bring a majority of people information about a new product or idea in a matter of days or even hours. Does that mean that a communications implant would have to appear and bring us to a state of equivalency to telepathy to achieve further increases in a rate of innovation? Or could this device bring with it an overwhelming size of information that people wouldn't be able to use it? Would a communications implant bring risks of instant propaganda, mind control by political and economic powers, computer virus equivalents that work in the human brain, or even a condition where the humans equipped with the device become a collective mind? That sounds like a science fiction movie if ever there was one and certainly represents an extreme. We could expect that a community mind would not support the differences necessary for people to be truly creative. The communications implant is literally here now. We already have people walking around carrying the precursor to a communications implant, which is their cellphones. Some are even equipped with wireless headphones. Often we see people walking around frequently with shiny colored blinking devices in their ears and it looks like they are talking to themselves. When you combine the blue-tooth earpiece with web browsing, and a video-capable cellphone, you are taking a step towards a complete communication implant. Glasses are also available that show a computer display to your eyes, while experiments have even been done in the use of stereo imagery to give a three-dimensional virtual reality experience. The technology has not been widely adopted yet and has no real use in society. The ultimate personal communication device can be expected to provide not just web access and video programming, but a complete out of this world experience. When the implant is linked directly to your body's nervous system, alternate reality could take on a whole new meaning. It could give a person instant diagnostics to what kind of sickness they may have. Stress levels could be monitored all the time in real time. Blood pressure, heart rates, and even calorie intake. This would revolutionize every choice we made about our health, and it would also serve to regulate our eating habits and fitness habits.

A lot of people are against combining technology to our bodies. Could we be half robot and half human someday with multiple implants that serve to make us better and more efficient? Is this next stage in our evolution? Only time will tell.

INDEPENDENT SOURCES

"Discovery Channel"

"*Huffington Post*"

Dictionary and Thesaurus — Merriam-Webster Online

Fox News

The Dalai Lama

CNN News

Wikipedia

TED Talks

The Young Turks

Yahoo News

Forbes

Nationalpriorities.org

HONORABLE MENTION

Active Duty & U.S Navy Veterans.
Damarilus Sowells
Jessica M. Mykel
Larry Elder
Joshua Pinz
Michael Doherty
Kevin Bright
Tracy Ford
Luis Antonio Roman Vega
Cory Rorex
David Ravenscroft
Tyler Diamond
Ashley Markoff
Tania Banks
Asif Azeez
Robert Duffy
Katherine McGraw
Erin M. Transue
Paul Badowski
Kevin Yeager
Luis Virola
Victor Galloway
Lonnie Harris

Shane Anderson
Robert W. Dickinson
Cory Ray
Sean Fierro
Pam Keksi
Cindy Ginder
Shane Anderson
Stephen Riggs
Thomas Proctor
Will Newlove
Zac Carrigan
Josh Simpson
Kayla Jordan
Ryan Tomei
Nicholas Herring
Nicholas Lewis
Kevin Kutsch
Thomas A. Delgado
Mike Croskey Murray
Peter Joseph Hicks
Luis Magana
Alisha McGinnis
Lyndzey Stovall
Nico Stovall

Ashley Byles
Randy Sorensen
Christopher Pollard
Daniel Logan
Donnell Stephens
Jonathan Triplett
David Maes
Adam Walko
Michael Childers
Galo J. Rodriguez
William Sharkey
Randy Wilfong
Aundrey Moore
Nicholas McCahill
Kelly Calliste
Joseph Prince
Chuck Mirelli
Ryan N Brannan
Chris Hinton
Kevin Stoudenmire

August Van Sickle
Aaron Kyle Jackson
Kristen Kurek
Bobby Simpson
E.J. Sheppard
Elizabeth Picray
Justin Snowden
Todd Horn
Bobby McMillin
Scott Allen Frederick
Duntrael Moss
Andrew Bolli
Matthew Eady
Kevin Simak
Chris Staley
David Coffer
Dan Metz
Frederick King
Shawn Steele

www.ingramcontent.com/pod-product-compliance
Ingram Content Group UK Ltd.
Pitfield, Milton Keynes, MK11 3LW, UK
UKHW041945230426
12048UKWH00008B/141